FOREWARD BY I

COMBATING JUVENILE DELINQUENCY

The Nouthetic Counselling Approach

ANENA MARIA GORETTI

AG PUBLISHING HOUSE

PRESENTED TO

_____

OCCASION

_____

PRESENTED BY

_____

DATE

_____

Copyright © Anena Maria Gorretti 2014

All rights reserved. No part of this publication may be produced, distributed, or transmitted in any form or by any means, including photocopying, recording, or other electronic or mechanical methods, without the prior writtenpermission of the publisher, except in the case of briefquoations embodied in the critical reviews and certain othernoncommercial uses permitted by copyright law.

Unless otherwise stated, all scripture quotations are taken from the Holy Bible, New Living Translation (NLT). Other versions cited are NIV, NKJV, AMP and KJV.Quotations marked NIV are taken from the HOLY BIBLE, NEW INTERNATIONAL VERSION.

Copyright © 1973, 1978, 1984 by International Bible Society. Used by permission of Hodder and Stoughton Ltd, a member of the Headline Plc Group. All right reserved. "NIV" is a registered trademark of International Bible Society. UK trademark number 1448790

Quotations marked KJV are from the Holy Bible, King James Version.

ISBN: 978-0-9576433-0-7

Cover design:
AG Publishing House

DEDICATION

To the youth of London Borough and their families, and to all others who are concerned about juvenile crime and the disintegration of the central family unit.

Contents

Dedication 5

Foreword 9

Acknowledgement 17

Chapter One

Introduction to Juvenile Deliquency 19

Chapter Two

Basic Assumptions of Delinquent Behaviour 29

Causes of and Conditions for the Formation
    of Delinquent Trajectories 34

Chapter Three

Basis for Nouthetic Counselling 47

The Commitment to Nouthetic Counselling 54

Chapter Four

Some General Principles and Practices in
    Nouthetic Counselling 62

Chapter Five

Forming and Adopting a Nouthetic
    Counselling Model 75

Homework—An Aid to Helping
    the Counsellee 107

Chapter Six

Counselling the Adolescent 114

Biblical Considerations and Applications
    Towards the Needs of Adolescents 124

Areas where Adolescents Face Their
    Greatest Problems 127

Chapter Seven

Youth Various Responses to Problems
    They Face....................................132

Suggestions For The Counsellor and Others
    Who Work With Adolescents..................134

Preventing Problems of the
    Adolescent Years 139

Chapter Eight

Counselling Angry, Unmotivated
    and Spiritually Indifferent Teenagers...........142

Chapter Nine

When Good Children Make Bad Choices 163

Helping Families with Twixters..................173

Chapter Ten

Closing Remarks 180

Chapter Eleven

The Riyadh Guidelines 185

References...................................203

FOREWORD

The problem of juvenile delinquency has become more complicated and universal. Crime prevention programmes are either ill-equipped to deal with the present realities or are non-existent. Many developing countries have done little or nothing to combat these problems, and international guidelines are obviously insufficient. Developed countries are engaged in activities aimed at juvenile crime prevention, but the overall effect of these is rather weak because the mechanisms in place are often inadequate to address the existing situation.

On the whole, current efforts to fight juvenile delinquency are characterized by the lack of systematic action and the absence of task-oriented and effective social work with both offenders and victims. Analysis is further complicated by a lack of international comparative data and a move away from the Almighty God. It is the job of all Christians to nurture the plan of God in all children.

Understanding that God has a plan for every life is a hard concept for many adults to grasp, let alone children who tend to question everything that is said to them. It is important to start teaching children from a young age that God has a plan for their lives and that they need to be open to hearing that Plan. Not leaving the task to simply explaining this concept to young people, as well as adults, but also working with them to help them discern God's plan, we will raise the next generation of children to be steadfast in their faith in Christ Jesus as their Lord and Saviour.

God has the best plan for your life! You could have come up with such a plan. The sooner you discover it, the better. It will lead you through life and help you be the best version of yourself. God made this plan for your life even before you were born, yet this doesn't mean that you will automatically walk in the plans He has for you, instead, He wants you to willingly surrender your will to Him, and for that, you need to come to the knowledge that, yes, indeed God has the best success plan for you.

"For I know the plans I have for you," declares the LORD, "plans to prosper you and not to harm you, plans to give you hope and a future." Jeremiah 29:11 (NIV)

"You have searched me, Lord, and you know me. You know when I sit and when I rise; you perceive my thoughts from afar. You discern my going out and my lying down; you are familiar with all my ways. Before a word is on my tongue you, Lord, know it completely.

You hem me in behind and before; you have laid your hand upon me.

Such knowledge is too wonderful for me, too lofty for me to attain. (Psalm 139:1-6) NIV.

For you created my inmost being; you knit me together in my mother's womb.

I praise you because I am fearfully and wonderfully made; your works are wonderful, I know that full well.

My frame was not hidden from you when I was made in the secret place, when I was woven together in the depths of the earth. Your eyes saw my unformed body; all the days ordained for me were written in your book before one of them came to be.

How precious to me are your thoughts, God!

How vast is the sum of them! Were I to count them, they would outnumber the grains of sand—when I awake, I am still with you." Psalm 139 (13-.18) NIV.

In order to fulfil God's plan, you must first of all have faith, and by faith I mean you must believe that God loves you, is wiser than you and that God is Almighty and can do everything.

There are three things you must believe about God, and it is very easy to believe them:

1. **That** God is Almighty and He can do anything, nothing is impossible for Him. It means He can arrange all the circumstances of your life for your good. Nobody can stop God's plan for your life. Why? Because God is Almighty. This is the first thing you must believe: God is Almighty."

2. **That** God loves you intensely. There is no one who loves you like God loves you. And because He loves you, He has really planned something good for you. Jesus said that if our earthly fathers "...know how to give good gifts to your children, how much more will your Heavenly Father in Heaven give good gifts to those who ask Him." Matt 7:11, Luke 11:13 (NIV). You know, people may think that 'if I give my whole life to God, it might be difficult'. That is the reason why some people don't surrender to God completely. They think "I can plan my life better". Why do you think that? Because you think God doesn't love you! That is untrue. When you trust God, you will be able to enjoy your life better, and things will go well with you.

3. That God's wisdom is greater than yours. Now these things are very easy to believe. You see, God knows all about the future, and you don't. You and I don't even know what's going to happen tomorrow let alone the farther future.

Believe that the God Who sees tomorrow and the next has a plan for your life. Events in your life, whether good or bad may come as a surprise to you, but is God surprised? Will God be surprised by why this happened to you? No."

It surely is best to trust our Heavenly Father, knowing that you are loved and your life is safe and secure in His Almighty hand. Yes, God does have a plan for you and if you want to know it, ask Him to reveal it to you. He surely will!

Galatians 6:1 gives us the command to restore another. This original word in the Greek was used by fishermen and physicians when they described the mending of fishnets and the setting of fractures. They both called their work "restoration". A torn net is of little or no value; the fish easily slip through and are lost. Likewise broken bones in the arm make it useless until they are set. Both nets and arms need to be restored to their original use.

God has given a heavy burden, and a broader authority that corresponds with it, to those who are official church counsellors. They must search out problems among the members of the church in order to care for them immediately. As shepherds, they are required not only to deal with the problems that they encounter on life's road, but to keep watch over the souls of every member (Hebrews 13:17). The pastor-counsellor is commanded to "keep watch" or to "remain awake and to be alert" to problems that may arise.

The ultimate goal of all restoration is to glorify God.

When we counsel another we must ask, "How has his relationship with Christ been affected by his problem?" This goal ought to guide one's method, attitudes and activities in helping the counsellee. Counsellors counsel not to punish, nor to gloat over the persons or to know their sin but help set them free from their problems and bring them into a closer and deeper relationship with the Lord. (I Corinthians 10:31, 32; Colossians 3:23).

All counselling has to do with changes in beliefs, judgments, values, relationships, thoughts, behaviour, and other such moral elements of life. Sin in human life has led to distortions of life in each of these categories. There is the resulting sinful thought and action that is the object of change in Christian counselling. The counsellor "aims" at straightening out the individual by changing his patterns of behaviour to conform to Biblical, God-given standards. The sinful responses are to be replaced with righteous ones.

There must be the element of concern or otherwise confrontation will be sterile, lifeless, cold, professional, harsh, and probably out of a critical spirit.

In this care for another there ought to be strong desire and untiring effort to relieve the person of the misery that sinful life patterns have brought upon him. The counsellor seeks to minister the Scriptures, to help the person interpret and apply the principles and practices of the Word of God in an attempt to help bring about the changes that will relieve him of his miseries and give him victory over his circumstances. Such a ministry is conducted prayerfully, in the power of the Holy Spirit. The counsellor will seek wisdom to minister the Scriptures with the goal of bringing change leading to restoration unto liberty in Christ Jesus.

As I commend **COMBATING JUVENILE DELINQUENCY with the Nouthetic Counselling Approach** to you, I leave the following instructions with you:

1. Pray that God will give you the ability to work with children to help them see God's Plan for everything in life. Whenever you are involved in a ministry activity, it is important to begin by asking for discernment in your own heart to ensure your intentions remain pure and God's Instructions are followed as clearly as possible.

2. Explain at the outset that God planned everything long before we were even born. Isaiah 25:1 (NIV) says "O Lord, you are my God; I will exalt you and praise your name, for in perfect faithfulness you have done marvellous things, things planned long ago." With every verse you plan to share, pray ahead of time that God will give you the answers for the question that are sure to be asked.

3. Discuss verses such as Ephesians 1:11 (NIV), "In him we were also chosen, having been predestined according to the plan of him who works out everything in conformity with the purpose of his will." This verse is a clear statement that God has a plan for all of His children. This is an excellent point to ask children to list some of their talents. No matter what age a person is, figuring out what talents God has given you is one of the first steps in finding God's path.

4. Ask the counsellee to look at their list of talents and come up with ways that they can accomplish God's purpose for their lives. Someone who loves

to write may say they could write Bible stories for other children. Another who enjoys singing may dream of being a professional singer. Yet another, who is good at building things, may begin to see that they can help people fix things. Consider the ages of the children concerned and help them to focus on God's plan for their lives.

5. Pray with the children (and their parents/carers) that God will help them find their path in life. Also pray that He will give the children the strength to stand up to peer pressure and anything which may draw them away from God's will. Make sure the children (and their parents/carers) know that you are always there for them to counsel them when they have questions.

Dr Tony Ogefere, JP

B.Ed(Hons) Counselling; BSc Psychology; MPhil Clinical Psychology; PhD Counselling Psychology, PgC. Citizenship, Leadership & Community Development; PgDip. Dual Diagnosis & PTSD Management

Registrar & Faculty Chair [2010 – 2012]

MATS, London (Off Campus, Minnesota Graduate School of Theology)

Registrar & Faculty Chair

The Light of the World Seminary

[UK Campus, Evangelical Theological Seminary, Orlando, Florida, USA]

Snr. Elder, The Light of the World Church, London

ACKNOWLEDGEMENT

Everyone would do better with a cheerleading team cheering them on, and my cheerleaders are sensational! They are:

- Rt. Rev (Dr) Ben Egbujor, President, Masters Academy and Theological Seminary, London, caring, optimistic, encouraging and always available to me. May God bless and continue to enlarge your coast.
- Dr Tony Ogefere, JP, Supervisor & Chair of Faculty, The Light of the World Seminary [UK Campus, Evangelical Theological Seminary, Orlando, Florida, USA] and my loving and wonderful talented Editor, the beam of light whose belief in and appreciation of my work fills my heart and makes me soar. For allowing me to reproduce extracts from his diary. God bless and keep you to see your children's children.
- Rev (Dr) Abraham and Rev (Mrs) Hannah Usikaro, my friends and mentors, who believe in my talents and applaud every step I take. I value and appreciate you dearly; may God bless you and remember all your good works.
- My daughter, Fiona Goretti and grandson, President Omari who constantly tell me that who I am makes a difference, and instil in me a joyous sense of purpose. The Lord will continue to be your sun and shield, and give you grace and glory: no good thing will He withhold from you.

- All the Leaders and members of Acts Ministries International Victory Chapel, thank you for your prayers, may God bless and prosper you in all that you do.
- June Coldwell for the administrative work. God will forever favour you and all that is yours.

It is no wonder that with so much loving energy behind me, the writing of this book flowed harmoniously and filled me with joy.

CHAPTER ONE

INTRODUCTION TO JUVENILE DELINQUENCY

For many young people today, traditional patterns guiding the relationships and transitions between family, school and work are being challenged. Social relations that ensure a smooth process of socialization are collapsing, and lifestyle trajectories are becoming more varied and less predictable. The restructuring of the labour market, the extension of the maturity gap (the period of dependence of young adults on the family) and, arguably, the more limited opportunities to become an independent adult are all changes influencing relationships with family and friends, educational opportunities and choices, labour market participation, leisure activities and lifestyles. It is not only developed countries that are facing this situation; in developing countries young people are experiencing new pressures as they undergo the transition from childhood to independence.

Rapid population growth, economic decline, the unavailability of housing and support services, poverty, unemployment and underemployment among youth, the decline in the authority of local communities, overcrowding in poor urban areas, the disintegration of the family, and ineffective educational systems are some of the pressures young people must deal with. Youths nowadays, regardless of gender, social origin or country of residence, are subject to individual risks but are also being presented with new individual challenges that may be beneficial or harmful. They sometimes become involved in illegal activities, become addicted to drugs, and use violence against their peers. Statistical data indicate that in virtually all parts of the world, with the exception of the United States, youth crime rates rose in the 1990s. In Western Europe, one of the few regions for which data are available, arrests of juvenile delinquents and under-age offenders increased by an average of about 50 per cent between the mid-1980s and the late 1990s. Countries in transition have also witnessed a dramatic rise in delinquency rates; since 1995, juvenile crime levels in many countries in Eastern Europe and the Commonwealth of Independent States have increased by more than 30 per cent. Many of the criminal offences are related to drug abuse and excessive alcohol use.

Majority of studies and programmes dealing with juvenile delinquency focus on youth offenders, however, adolescents are also victims of criminal or delinquent acts. The continuous threat of victimization is having a serious impact on the socialization of young men and on their internalization of the norms and values of the larger society. According to data on crimes registered by the police, more than 80 per cent of all violent incidents are not reported by the victims. Information about the victims allows conclusions to be drawn about the offenders as well. Results of self-report studies indicate that an overwhelming majority of those who participate in violence against young people are about the same age and gender as their victims; in most cases the offenders are males acting in groups. Those most likely to be victims of violence are between the ages of 16 and 19. Within this age group, 91 in every 1,000 become victims of violence. Surveys have shown that men are more likely than women to become victims. In the United States, 105 in every 1,000 men become crime victims, compared with 80 per 1,000 women. Men are 2.5 times more likely to be victims of aggravated assault. Older people are less often affected; as mentioned, crimes are usually committed by representatives of the same age groups to which the victims belong. Young people who are at risk of becoming delinquent often live in difficult circumstances. Children who for various reasons—including parental alcoholism, poverty, breakdown of the family, overcrowding, abusive conditions in the home, the growing HIV/AIDS scourge, or the death of parents during armed conflicts—are orphans or unaccompanied and are without the means of subsistence, housing and other basic necessities are at the greatest risk of falling into juvenile delinquency. The number of children in especially difficult circumstances is estimated to have increased from 100 million to 180 million between 2000 and 2011.

Despite vast technological advances visible in all countries today, the processes for helping children and youth into mature adulthood still present a challenge for parents, youth workers and communities as a whole.

By looking at the painstaking efforts of the professionals—teachers, social workers, judges, psychologists, sociologists, psychiatrists—who seek to find ways and means to prevent and control the wayward behaviour of youth, it becomes apparent that the professionals cannot solve or even control the delinquency problem by themselves. Every citizen and every parent must share this task, and, we must involve youths themselves in the solution to what has become a youth plague.

This book has been prepared for parents, interested citizens (including community leaders), and older youths who want to understand and help those youngsters whose behaviour has brought them to the attention of the local authorities, the courts and crime prevention officials. It emphasises the need to define and differentiate the delinquent and reviews a variety of approaches which may be adopted in helping youth offenders. These approaches generally reflect a causative, diagnostic, and rehabilitative orientation.

In practice, however, many prevention approaches have proved to be ineffective. Studies show that shock incarceration (boot camp) does not reduce criminality. Short-term, "quick fix" job training has not lowered arrest rates. Neither traditional psychotherapy nor behaviour modification has shown great promise as a vehicle for redirecting delinquent and criminal youth to restoration. Evidence has shown that some methods—in particular, scare-oriented approaches or programmes that place groups of delinquent youth together for extended treatment—have actually worsened the behaviour of its participants.

Experience shows that efforts to tackle gang membership are the most ineffective. Several techniques for transforming the gang culture environment have been suggested, but they tend to deal only with the criminal aspect of the problem, while the socio-economic and other conditions and circumstances that compel juveniles to enter a gang remain forgotten. Further, traditional social institutions are rarely engaged in the process. Nevertheless, programmes designed to address the problem of gang membership have been implemented, and many of them are reported to be successful by some evaluators and completely inadequate by others. According to some researchers, the implementation and positive appraisal of a number of initiatives can be attractive to politicians who wish to demonstrate that they are tackling the problem of juvenile delinquency. Such political considerations make adequate evaluation of prevention work difficult in many cases, with the result that ineffective programmes may continue to operate while the problems of juvenile delinquency remain unsolved. It must, however, be acknowledged that the expenditure of large sums of money and resources can be thoughtlessly imitative while such resources achieve little or no return and do little to solve the problem. A proactive but carefully considered approach to the development and implementation of prevention and rehabilitation programmes is needed, with care taken to apply those lessons learned through direct experience. Research and evaluation must therefore be integrated into all prevention efforts.

With the statistics revealing an increase in murder, illicit sex, and callous disregard for life and property, something has gone terribly wrong. What causes our young people to lash out against life with fierce brutality? Disintegrating families and the increase in light-speed technology provide fertile ground for relational alienation. Societal ties and foundational doctrines have crumbled in the face of post modernism, leaving our youth feeling lost and disconnected. Violence ensues as an outgrowth of their unbearable pain, loneliness, and confusion. At the root of this pain is a sense of alienation and aloneness. If we are to counter it, we must offer our youth strong relational connections. The stronger the connections, the better equipped they will be to make positive life choices and lead healthy lives.

Why? What causes young people to resort to violence towards their peers, parents, teachers and society at large? What is happening in our culture that produces such vicious anger in children?

Today, computers can be programmed as virtual reality simulators, offering hands-on instruction on everything from driving a car to piloting an airplane. Similar technology used to develop realistic, interactive video games is teaching our young people how to kill. Points are given for hitting specific targets; in many popular games, headshots are rewarded with bonus points!

The problems we are seeing are not solely outgrowths of violent video games, however; a major factor is the abandonment of moral absolutes. Establishing a foundation of unwavering truths, the moral absolutes identified in Scripture, is the key to curbing the destructive trends among our youth. There is something even deeper still, the need to feel connected to parents, to adults in general, and to society as a whole. Feeling alienated in a hostile world is frightening and the resulting emotional pain often unleashes anti-social behaviours.

To successfully reach out to this "disconnected generation," it is imperative that we learn who these children are and why they feel so alone.

In the quest for a unique identity, each generation creates new social norms by pushing back existing cultural boundaries. The present generation, often referred to as "echo boomers," "millennia's" or "mosaics," number over 22 million. These "baby boomer offspring" enjoy unprecedented opportunities, including almost limitless access to the world through the Internet.

Social relationships that once revolved around family, church, school and friends now take place through cyberspace chat rooms, e-mail, and instant messages.

Violent interactive video games, rejection of moral absolutes, and cyberspace technology have all been contributing factors in widening the present generation gap. Add increasing divorce rates and the growing numbers of children coming home from school to empty houses, and we can begin to grasp the underlying causes for their disconnection.

It is not what you say that matters; it is what you mean. In many homes, teenagers and parents are failing to connect because they simply do not understand one another.

"I'm talking about adults and youth using a common vocabulary with different definitions, completely unaware that such differences exist."

The root cause of this communication problem is the fact that the thinking of many teenagers has been coloured by the modern cultural doctrine of post- modernism woven into the fabric of their lives via public education, secular music, television, advertising, movies, and peers.

Words like tolerance, acceptance and truth have been subtly redefined. A post-modern thinker cannot separate a person from his or her beliefs and actions. Therefore, criticism of any aspect of a teenager's life strikes a blow at his self-esteem and causes feelings of rejection.

"Post-modernists contend that anyone who claims to hold an objective truth that unfavourably judges the values, beliefs, or lifestyle of another person is intolerant and bigoted."

The greatest deception, however, is the belief that there is no objective truth true for everyone, everywhere, all the time. Subtle cultural conditioning has convinced our youth that they can create a personal lifestyle that is "true," even when it violates Biblical mandates. Dedicated Christian parents, committed to raising their children to respect and obey God, experience challenges in trying to understand why their children struggle to embrace their traditional values. Frustrated teenagers cannot understand why mother and father will not let them choose their own beliefs. And the distance between them widens.

"The real challenge before us is learning how to relate to our children's sometimes complex and confusing world and make relational connections at a deep, emotional level that no cultural influence will be able to destroy."

Disconnection can arise as a result of the generation gap and the influence of post-modernism, but it does not have to result in isolation and destruction. Parents, youth workers, local authorities, communities, pastors, and Christian educators can reach across that gap to build strong, permanent connections. Given Paul's teaching on the rejection of the first two commandments as the cause of ethical chaos, we must recognise that the key to the Christian reconstruction of society is the preaching of the Gospel. Indeed, the twin pillars of the Calvinist wing of the Reformation are the Biblical doctrine of salvation (i.e. justification by faith alone) and Biblical worship. A society will not and cannot be moral apart from believing in Christ and worshiping Him according to Scripture. Any attempt by society at social reform apart from preaching Christ and teaching how God is to be truthfully worshiped is in vain.

CHAPTER TWO

BASIC ASSUMPTIONS OF DELINQUENT BEHAVIOUR

It is impossible to develop effective prevention programmes without understanding the causal link between juvenile involvement and criminal activity. Different approaches are used in scientific and practical literature on juvenile crime and violence to define and explain the delinquent behaviour of young people. To criminologists, juvenile delinquency encompasses all public wrongs committed by young people between the ages of 12 and 20. Sociologists take a broader view, asserting that it covers a multitude of different violations of legal and social norms, from minor offences to serious crimes, committed by juveniles. Included under the umbrella of juvenile delinquency are status offences, so-called because they are closely linked with the age range of the offender; a particular action or behaviour is considered a violation of the law only if it is committed by a juvenile (examples include truancy and absconding from home). In an attempt to explain the theoretical underpinnings of delinquency, sociologists associate the elements of youth behaviour with the home, family, neighbourhood, peers and other variables which, together or separately, positively or negatively, influence the formation of young people's social environment.

Antisocial behaviour has been considered by society as a normal part of growing up or the beginning of a long-term pattern of criminal activity. The United Nations Guidelines for the Prevention of Juvenile Delinquency (the Riyadh Guidelines) assert that "youthful behaviour or conduct which does not conform to overall social norms and values is often part of the maturation and growth process and tends to disappear spontaneously in most individuals with the transition to adulthood". The majority of young people who commit some kind of petty offence at some point during their adolescence do not turn their criminal activity into a career in the long term. However, while delinquency appears to be a common characteristic of the transition period and process of becoming an adult, it is important to note that some juveniles form criminal links with a corresponding subculture and engage in the activities of adult criminal groups, in effect choosing delinquent careers.

Statistical data in many countries show that delinquency is largely a group phenomenon; between two-thirds and three-quarters of all juvenile offences are committed by members of various groups. Even those juveniles who commit offences alone are likely to be associated with groups. According to data from the Russian Federation, the rate of criminal activity among juveniles in groups is about three to four times higher than that of adult offenders. Juvenile group crime is most prevalent among 14-year olds and least prevalent among 17-year-olds. The rates are higher for theft, robbery and rape, and lower for premeditated murder and grievous bodily harm.

Similarities in the basic characteristics of juvenile group behaviour are found in almost every class and cultural context. Juvenile peer groups are noted for their high levels of social cohesiveness, hierarchical organization, and a certain codes of behaviour based on the rejection of adult values and experience. The subcultural aspect of juvenile group activities is rarely given the consideration which is needed. Different juvenile groups adopt what is considered to be a heterogeneous mix, or synthesis, of predominant (class-based) values, which are enhanced by the entertainment industry, are inter-generational (group-based) values, and which are native to the family or community. Subcultures can be defined as particular lifestyle systems that are developed in groups and are in structurally subordinate positions as a result of pressure exerted by the predominant systems.

Subcultures reflect individual and group attempts to solve societal and structural contradictions. One of the most important aspects of subcultures is that they form patterns of behaviour that have substantial symbolic value for the individuals involved. Currently there are various subcultures in which deviant behaviour and violence play an important role. Some groups and subcultures use violence as a means of solving interpersonal conflicts, and the ensuing environment created is an important factoring contributing to delinquent or criminal behaviour. This might even be referred to as a subculture of violence, in which aggression is considered an acceptable approach to problem-solving. Those most likely to participate in such activities are usually members of territorial gangs. Studies reveal that the most frequent offences committed by gang members are fighting, street extortion and school violence.

The role of juvenile groups in communities must be taken into consideration. A community is defined by the similar social characteristics of its residents, such as membership in a social class or ethnic group. Urban neighbourhood communities provide their members with a certain everyday social comfort at the local level. Under conditions of social diversity and urban growth these neighbourhood units, like rural communities, are able to balance the social interests of the groups they contain.

Membership in juvenile groups is sometimes an essential element of socialization. Several studies have shown the possibility of establishing connections between delinquent groups and other social institutions—a "symbiosis" in which gangs can, for instance, work to satisfy any of a community's needs. As mentioned earlier, in many cases juvenile delinquent groups are also the entry point to adult organized crime.

Available data show that delinquency and crime have strong gender associations. Records indicate that the crime rates of male juvenile and male young adult offenders are more than double those of young females, and conviction rates are six or seven times higher. The number of male juvenile suspects for every 100,000 members of the designated age group is more than six times the corresponding figure for females; for those in the youth category, the male-female suspect ratio is even higher, at 12.5 to 1.[6] There appear to be a number of reasons why more young men than young women become involved in violent or criminal behaviour. Various restrictive and stimulative factors encourage women to conform to social norms that do not apply to men, one example being the fear of sexual assault. Girls are subject to stronger family control than are boys. Cultural concepts are such that society at large is less tolerant of deviant behaviour among young women than among young men. In addition, aggression and violence play an important role in the construction of masculinity and sexuality in patriarchal societies, the primary objective being to reinforce and maintain the status and authoritative position of men. The male perception of violence can be minimized, forgiven, denied or justified. Men often do not consider such acts as verbal or sexual insults to constitute violent behaviour. There are cultures in which the dominant type of masculinity is more or less openly directed towards violent confrontation, domination and control. And there others in which the socialization of young males towards hegemonic masculinity is not attached to norms of physical prowess, hard work and a readiness to fight. Nonetheless, for both boys and girls, the street gang is an ideal context for "doing gender" (establishing gender differences).

Consequently, girls who are gang members are not simply passive recipients of "patriarchy" but active participants in the construction of gender relations. The peer group plays an important part in the construction of gender roles and relations, including delinquent behaviour. Youth gangs reflect the gender-based power relations in society and the related discourse and practices by which they are reproduced. Consequently, differences in male and female behaviour in this context appear to stem partly from a product of the social construction of gendered dominance and subordination in gang arrangements.

CAUSES OF AND CONDITIONS FOR THE FORMATION OF DELINQUENT TRAJECTORIES

The intensity and severity of juvenile offences are generally determined by the social, economic and cultural conditions prevailing in a country.

There is evidence of a universal increase in juvenile crime occurring concurrently with economic decline, particularly in the poor districts of large cities. In many cases, street children later go on to become young offenders, having already encountered violence in their immediate social environment as either witnesses or victims of violent acts. The educational attainments of this group tend to be rather low as a rule, basic social experience acquired in the family is often insufficient, and the socio-economic environment is determined by poverty and under/un-employment.

The causes of and conditions for juvenile crime are usually found at each level of the social structure, including society as a whole, social institutions, social groups and organizations, and interpersonal relations. Juveniles' choice of delinquent careers and the consequent perpetuation of delinquency are fostered by a wide range of factors, the most important of which are described below.

ECONOMIC AND SOCIAL FACTORS

Juvenile delinquency is driven by the negative consequences of social and economic development, particularly, economic crises, political instability, and the weakening of major institutions (including the State, systems of public education and public assistance, and the family). Socio-economic instability is often linked to persistent unemployment and low incomes among the young which can increase the likelihood of their involvement in criminal activity.

CULTURAL FACTORS

Delinquent behaviour often occurs in social settings in which the norms for acceptable behaviour have broken down. Under such circumstances, many of the common rules that deter people from committing socially unacceptable acts may lose their relevance for some members of society. They respond to the traumatizing and destructive changes in the social reality by engaging in rebellious, deviant or even criminal activities. An example of such a setting would be the modernization of traditional societies and the accompanying changes wrought by the application of new technologies; shifts of this magnitude affect the types and organization of labour activity, social characteristics, lifestyles and living arrangements, and these changes, in turn, affect authority structures, forms of obedience, and modes of political participation—even going so far as to influence perceptions of reality.

In both developed and developing countries, consumer standards created by the media are considerably beyond the capacity of most families to achieve. Nevertheless, these ideals become a virtual reality for many young people, some of whom will go to great lengths to maintain a lifestyle they cannot afford. For the reason that not all population groups have access to the necessary resources, including education, professional training, satisfactory employment and income, health services, and adequate housing, there are those who are unable to achieve their goals by legal means. The contradiction between idealized and socially approved goals and the sometimes limited real-life opportunities to achieve them legally creates a sense of frustration in many young people. A criminal career becomes one form of addressing this contradiction. One of the reasons for delinquent behaviour is therefore an excessive focus on proposed goals (achieving success) coupled with insufficient means to achieve them.

The likelihood of deviant acts occurring in this context depends in many respects not only on the unavailability of legal opportunities but also on the level of access to illegal opportunities. Some juveniles, cognizant of the limitations imposed by legal behaviour, come under the influence of adult criminals. Many young people retreat into the confines of their own groups and resort to drug use for psychological or emotional escape. The use of alcohol and illegal drugs by juveniles is one cause of delinquency, as they are often compelled to commit crimes (usually theft) to obtain the cash needed to support their substance use.

Urbanization

Geographical analysis suggests that countries with more urbanized populations have higher registered crime rates than do those with strong rural lifestyles and communities. This may be attributed to the differences in social control and social cohesion. Rural groupings rely mainly on family and community control as a means of dealing with antisocial behaviour and exhibit markedly lower crime rates. Urban industrialized societies tend to resort to formal legal and judicial measures, an impersonal approach that appears to be linked to higher crime rates. Cultural and institutional differences are such that responses to the same offence may vary widely from one country to another.

The ongoing process of urbanization in developing countries is contributing to juvenile involvement in criminal behaviour. The basic features of the urban environment foster the development of new forms of social behaviour deriving mainly from the weakening of primary social relations and control, increasing reliance on the media at the expense of informal communication, and the tendency towards anonymity. These patterns are generated by the higher population density, degree of heterogeneity, and numbers of people found in urban contexts.

FAMILY

Studies show that children who receive adequate parental supervision are less likely to engage in criminal activities. Dysfunctional family settings—characterized by conflict, inadequate parental control, weak internal linkages and integration, and premature autonomy—are closely associated with juvenile delinquency. Children in disadvantaged families that have few opportunities for legitimate employment and face a higher risk of social exclusion are overrepresented among offenders. The plight of ethnic minorities and migrants, including displaced persons and refugees in certain parts of the world, is especially distressing. The countries in transition are facing particular challenges in this respect, with the associated insecurity and turmoil contributing to an increase in the numbers of children and juveniles neglected by their parents and suffering abuse and violence at home. The family as a social institution is currently undergoing substantial changes; its form is diversifying with, for example, the increase in one-parent families, non-marital unions and homosexual unions and adoptions. The absence of fathers in many low-income families can lead boys to seek patterns of masculinity in delinquent groups of peers. These groups in many respects substitute for the family, define male roles, and contribute to the acquisition of such attributes as cruelty, strength, excitability and anxiety.

The importance of family well-being is becoming increasingly recognized. Success in school depends greatly on whether parents have the capacity to provide their children with "starting" opportunities (including the resources to buy books and manuals and pay for studies). Adolescents from low-income families often feel excluded. To raise their self-esteem and improve their status they may choose to join a juvenile delinquent group. These groups provide equal opportunities to everyone, favourably distinguishing themselves from school and family, where positions of authority are occupied by adults. When young people are exposed to the influence of adult offenders they have the opportunity to study delinquent behaviour, and the possibility of their engaging in adult crime becomes more real. The "criminalization" of the family also has an impact on the choice of delinquent trajectories. A study carried out in prisons in the United States reveals that families involved in criminal activities tend to push their younger members towards violating the law. More than two-thirds of those interviewed had relatives who were incarcerated; for 25 percent it was a father and for another 25 percent a brother or sister.

MIGRATION

Because immigrants often exist in the margins of society and the economy, and have little chance of success in the framework of the existing legal order, they often seek comfort in their own environment and culture. Differences in norms and values and the varying degrees of acceptability of some acts in different ethnic subcultures result in cultural conflicts, which are one of the main sources of criminal behaviour. Native urban populations tend to perceive immigrants as obvious deviants.

THE MEDIA

Television and movies have popularized the "cult of heroes", which promotes justice through the physical elimination of enemies. Many researchers have concluded that young people who watch violence tend to behave more aggressively or violently, particularly when provoked. This is mainly characteristic of 8- to 12-year-old boys, who are more vulnerable to such influences. The media introduces violence to an individual in one or more of the following three methods: the first of which is through movies that demonstrate violent acts and excite the audience. The negative influence can be unconsciously transferred into everyday life, pushing an individual to engage in hostile and violent physical activity on the streets. This type of influence is temporary, lasting from several hours to several days. Secondly, television can portray ordinary daily violence committed by parents or peers (the imposition of penalties for failing to study or for violations of certain rules or norms of conduct). It is impossible to find television shows that do not portray such patterns of violence, because viewer approval of this type of programming has ensured its perpetuation. As a result, children are continually exposed to the use of violence in different situations—and the number of violent acts on television appears to be increasing. Thirdly, violence depicted in the media is unreal and has a surrealistic quality; wounds bleed less, and the real pain and agony resulting from violent actions are very rarely shown, so the consequences of violent behaviour often seem negligible. Over time, television causes a shift in the system of human values and indirectly leads children to view violence as a desirable and even courageous way of re-establishing justice. The American Psychological Association has reviewed the evidence and has concluded that television violence accounts for about 10 per cent of aggressive behaviour among children.

EXCLUSION

The growing gap between rich and poor has led to the emergence of "unwanted others". The exclusion of some people is gradually increasing with the accumulation of obstacles, ruptured social ties, unemployment and identity crises. Welfare systems that have provided relief but have not eliminated the humble socio-economic position of certain groups, together with the increased dependence of low-income families on social security services, have contributed to the development of a "new poor" class in many places.

The symbolic exclusion from society of juveniles who have committed even minor offences has important implications for the development of delinquent careers. Studies show that the act of labelling may lead to the self-adoption of a delinquent image, which later results in delinquent activity.

YOUTH INFLUENCE

Youth policies seldom reflect an understanding of the role of the peer group as an institution of socialization. Membership in a delinquent gang, like membership in any other natural grouping, can be part of the process of becoming an adult. Through such primary associations, an individual acquires a sense of safety and security, develops knowledge of social interaction, and can demonstrate such qualities as loyalty or leadership. In "adult" society, factors such as social status, private welfare, race and ethnicity are of great value; however, all members of adolescent groups are essentially in an equal position and have similar opportunities for advancement in the hierarchical structure. In these groups, well-being depends wholly on personal qualities such as strength, will and discipline. Quite often delinquent groups can counterbalance or compensate for the imperfections of family and school. A number of studies have shown that juvenile gang members consider their group a family. For adolescents constantly facing violence, belonging to a gang can provide protection within the neighbourhood. In some areas those who are not involved in gangs continually face the threat of assault, oppression, harassment or extortion on the street or at school. As one juvenile from London said, "I became involved in a gang when I was about 13 years old, but I joined it only when I was 15 years of age. I had a girlfriend and I feared for her, and the gang was able to provide for her safety."

DELINQUENT IDENTITIES

In identifying the causes of criminal behaviour, it is important to determine which factors contribute to a delinquent identity and why some adolescents who adopt a delinquent image do not discard that image in the process of becoming an adult. Delinquent identity is quite complex and is, in fact, an overlay of several identities linked to delinquency itself and to a person's ethnicity, race, class and gender. Delinquent identity is always constructed as an alternative to the conventional identity of the larger society. Violence and conflict are necessary elements in the construction of such group and delinquent identities. The foundations of group identity and activity are established and strengthened through the maintenance of conflict relations with other juvenile groups and society as a whole. Violence appear to, prima facie, integrate members into a group, reinforcing their sense of identity, and thereby hastening the process of group adaptation to the local environment.

Other factors that may provide motivation for joining a gang are the possibilities of economic and social advancement. In many socio-cultural contexts the delinquent way of life has been romanticized to a certain degree, and joining a gang is one of the few channels of social mobility available for disadvantaged youth. According to one opinion, urban youth gangs have a stabilizing effect on communities characterized by a lack of economic and social opportunities.

Offenders and Victims

Criminal activity can be said, in some circumstances, to be a causal link with a victim's behaviour. Often times, behavior can be linked with criminal activity. In some circumstances, a person's behavior can be an indication to whether or not they will participate in criminal activity or become a victim. In the offender's view, a victim's reaction can be seen as provoking the offender. However, "appropriate" behaviour may prevent a criminal act or at least minimize its impact. According to scientific literature, the likelihood of becoming a victim is related to the characteristics or qualities of a person, a social role or a social situation that provoke or facilitate criminal behaviour; personal characteristics such as individual or family status, financial prosperity, and safety, as well as logistical characteristics such as the time and place in which a confrontation occurs, can also determine the extent of victimization. 'Accidental' victims usually arise where the assault or offending act is preceded by heated discussion. According to the classification of psychological types, there are three types of typical adolescent victims of violence: accidental victims; people predisposed to become victims; and "inborn" victims. Studies have shown that in the majority of cases that result in bodily harm, the offender and his victim are acquainted with one another and may be spouses, relatives or friends; this is said to be true for 80 percent of murders and 70 percent of sexual crimes.

CHAPTER THREE

BASIS FOR NOUTHETIC COUNSELLING

I. BRINGING RESTORATION

What is nouthetic counselling? The answer is simple and yet very profound. While the work of nouthetic counselling is not necessarily easy, it is very much needed. It is the process by which a Christian restores another person to a place of usefulness to Christ in His Church. The command in the Word of God is very clear that we "restore" any brothers or sisters whom God providentially places in our pathway daily.

Galatians 6:1 gives us the command to restore another. This original word in the Greek was used by fishermen and physicians when they described the mending of fishnets and the setting of fractures. They both called their work "restoration". A torn net is of little or no value; the fish easily slip through and are lost. Likewise broken bones in the arm make it useless until they are set. Both nets and arms need to be restored to their original use.

God has given a heavy burden, and a broader authority that corresponds with it to those who are official church counsellors. They must search out problems among the members of the church in order to care for them immediately. As shepherds they are required not only to handle their own problems but to keep watch over the soul of every member (Hebrews 13:17). The pastor-counsellor is commanded to "keep watch" or to "remain awake and to be alert" to problems that may arise.

The ultimate goal of all restoration is to glorify God. When we counsel another we must ask, "How has his usefulness to Christ been diminished by his problem?" The goal ought to guide one's method, attitudes and activities in helping the counsellee. We counsel not to punish, gloat over the persons or to know their sin. We desire to bring them to usefulness and victory in the Lord (I Corinthians 10:31, 32; Colossians 3:23).

II. Giving "Nouthetic" Counselling:

A. Christ is at the centre of all true counselling:

1. All things were created by Jesus Christ (Colossians 1:16, 17).
2. It was God through Christ who formed man out of the dust of the ground (Genesis 2:7).
3. The Lord specifically and intricately designed every single body differently (Psalm 139:13-16).

B. Nouthetic Counselling is the work of every Christian: (Romans 15:14; 15:1; Galatians 6:1; Colossians 3:16).

1. Paul counselled nouthetically on a one-to-one basis (Acts 20:31).

2. Every Christian, who is spiritual, who is Spirit-filled should be involved in the work of counselling.

C. Nouthetic Counselling includes at least three elements:

The word, nouthetic, comes from the Greek word *-nouthesia*. It is simply a designation for Biblical counselling. It is a comprehensive term which denotes a use of the Scriptures foremost in the counselling process. The Greek word "nouthesia" has often been translated "admonish, warn, and teach." A. T. Robertson, a Greek authority, has translated it "to put sense into" also translated "counsel." Jay Adams translates it "nouthetic" because no one English word in itself defines it.

Jay Adams gives the following: "It contains the three elements: *change* **through** *confrontation* **out of** *concern*. It presupposes:

- that there are sinful patterns and activities in the life of the counsellee that God desires to be *changed*.
- that this change will be brought about through a verbal *confrontation* of the counsellee with the Scriptures as the counsellor ministers them in the power of the Holy Spirit.
- that this confrontation is done in a loving, **caring**, familial manner for the benefit of the counsellee. There is deep *concern*.

III. Some Basic Elements in Nouthetic Counselling:

Nouthetic counselling suggests that there is something wrong with the person who is to be confronted nouthetically, or Biblically. It arises out of the fact that there is a condition which God desires changed. The fundamental purpose of nouthetic confrontation then is to effect personality and behavioural change—conformity to the image of Christ. God requires change: All counselling aims at change. Without this element whatever we might be doing, it is not counselling. In the word, "restore" we had a term which required change. Usefulness was lost. The change must take place because of the Christian who is caught in sin (Galatians 6:1). The change that is contemplated in the restoration to usefulness is a change in life patterns in which sinful beliefs, attitudes, and behaviours are replaced by righteous ones (Ephesians 4:22-24).

A. All counselling has to do with changes in beliefs, judgments, values, relationships, thoughts, behaviour, and other such moral elements of life. Sin in human life has led to distorted perceptions in each of these categories. There is the resulting sinful thought and action that is the object of change in Christian counselling. The counsellor "aims" at straightening out the individual by changing his patterns of behaviour to conform to Biblical standards. The sinful responses are to be replaced with righteous ones.

B. Biblical counselling must aim for preventive counselling. If we would labour in this area both in teaching and preaching, many of the problems people face would be alleviated in the first place.

C. Problems are solved by verbal means, that is, there must be some Biblical confrontation of the problem at hand. This implies personal, verbal contact in which the Word of God is applied to the counsellee. There is no form of nastiness, or harshness, or a know-it-all-attitude in the concept of biblical *confrontation.* There is training by the mouth, that is, it is a person-to-person verbal use of Scripture, sometimes by encouragement and sometimes by reproof. There must be a "speaking of the truth in love", a truth telling that pleases God (Ephesians 4:15, 25).

D. There must be the element of concern or otherwise confrontation will be sterile, lifeless, cold, professional, harsh, and probably out of a critical spirit. In this care for another, there ought to be a strong desire and an untiring effort to relieve the person of the misery that sinful life patterns have brought upon him. This is true nouthetic counselling.

The counsellor seeks to minister through the Scriptures, to help the person interpret and apply the principles and practices of the Word of God in an attempt to help bring about the changes that will relieve him of his miseries. Such a ministry is conducted prayerfully, in the power of the Holy

Spirit. The counsellor will seek wisdom to minister the Scriptures with the goal to bring change which will lead to restoration unto usefulness.

The counsellor will steer the counselling process toward change in the direction of greater conformity to Biblical principles and practices. The goal must be to meet the obstacles or sin problems as the Holy Spirit directs, helping the person to understand the problem. The purpose is God's glory in the life of the counsellee

E. Nouthetic counselling may be defined in short as

1. meeting the person where he is;
2. pointing out what is wrong; and
3. helping him obtain the desirable personality and behavioural change—based upon Scripture.

This will also necessitate helping him to understand his sinful thinking that produces the actions.

F. Nouthetic Counselling is always Biblical counselling:
In II Timothy 3:16- 17, we find the ultimate purpose of the Word of God in the life of every Christian. Not only is the Word of God given to make us wise unto salvation and to be the instrument God uses to bring this about (I Peter 2:23; Titus 3:5), but also He would use it to bring about sanctification in daily life.

According to II Timothy 3:15-17, as we use the Word of God it becomes to the counsellee:

1. **Doctrine**—by which we know truth and the truth shall set you free (John 8:32, 36).
2. **Reproof**– by which we compare our lives with the Biblical standard, and become aware of our sinful condition through conviction. Without conviction there will never be change. A convicting activity must be pursued when the counsellee is unaware of his sin or is still unrepentant. The Holy Spirit must work the conviction in the life of the counsellee as the counsellor presents the Word of God (James 1: 19-25).
3. **Correction**- by which we recognize the change needed and begin to bring about that change. Repentance leads to a change in behaviour through a change of mind and will take place through correction by the Word of God. This activity is "to set straight" in which we show the counsellee how to break sinful habits and how to overcome failures and weaknesses. This includes reconciliation, restitution and putting on new patterns.
4. **Instruction**- Scriptures bring instruction in righteousness. Through the Word of God we recognize how far we have fallen short of God's plan and how sin brings much misery. The instructing activity will provide instruction concerning putting off the old ways and putting on the new, and about staying out of sin in the future.
5. **Discipline- in righteousness**. This structuring activity will involve laying out a personal

Biblical pattern of living to replace the old, through **regular Bible study, and the ministration of the Word of God.**

THE COMMITMENT TO NOUTHETIC COUNSELLING:

I. THE CASE FOR PASTORAL COUNSELLING:

We have seen that the Scriptures were given to us… for doctrine, for reproof, for correction, and for instruction in righteousness (II Timothy 3:16, 17). The Bible is the book God has provided to guide us in counselling and it includes all that is needed to bring about the change required to live a life pleasing to God. Surely that very fact should cause us to realize the importance of the Pastor's involvement with counselling. .

A. The Definition of Pastoral Counselling:

A pastor is a shepherd, elder and overseer. He is a mature Christian chosen by God to watch over his people. His appointment and ordination is recognition of the Divine Call upon his life. His responsibilities include evangelizing (II Timothy 4:5), leading by example (Peter 5:3), teaching, admonishing, correct, training, edifying, and restoring. His primary ministry is the preaching and teaching of the Word of God (II Timothy 4:2). But in the midst of all of this is the very important ministry of counselling.

The designation "pastoral counselling" is limited primarily to the pastoral use of the Word of God in restoring sick or distressed members of the flock of God. Such counselling involves a decision to deal with an individual to alleviate his distress in a particular way. It is to help the person think differently, Biblically and feel differently about a whole area or several areas of his life. It is the use of the Word of God to bring about change in the person's thinking, feeling, and actions, and to help him achieve a personal experience of the abundant life that Christ promised (John 10:10).

B. The Lack of Pastoral Counselling:

While many Biblical Pastors know there is a great need for counseling, some have yet to take on the responsibility. Others are troubled with thoughts of incompetence when they face the strange theories and vocabulary of psychology and the great variety of psychotherapies (the secular approach). They are unsure of their ability to master the subject of counselling well enough to be of any practical application. Furthermore, they have assumed the greater discomfort of understanding how to counsel without the application of secular methods. But instead of all these concerns, their principal objective should be attaining expertise in the use of the Word of God because it is the greatest of therapeutic agents.

C. Arguments for Pastoral counselling:

1. *The Word of God is very clear about the great needs that people face which affect them mentally, emotionally, and physically.* We cannot get away from the fact that Biblical Psychology exists and it is a legitimate study. (Psalm 42, 43) Throughout the history of Christianity, Pastors and Spiritual leaders have sought to understand the workings of the troubled mind in order to more skillfully apply the Word of God as a means of relief.

2. *Pastors are the major source of counselling.* The Pastor is often the first, and sometimes the only, professional person to whom people go for comfort and counsel. Surveys prove that 42% of the people with problems would prefer to seek out a Pastor. The Pastor has the kind of ready-made atmosphere for counselling that most others do not have.

3. *We must have emotionally well people who are mature if we are to also have evangelism.* Christian maturity is a basic requirement for service. Emotionally ill saints do not win many souls. Depressed and defeated Christians are likely to provoke the unconverted to turn away from Christ or Christianity. We must edify the saints if we are to help them qualify for service and outreach.

4. *Tremendous needs do exist among the saints of God.* **Probably every failure and/or sin experienced by the unconverted has also been experienced by God's people.** The Word of

God has much counsel about such things as anxiety, depression, fear, jealousy, anger, sexual sins, marriage failures, frustration and resentment, etc. **In almost every instance these problems involve sinful behaviour and irrational thinking.**

a. There is the **worried, anxious and fearful person** who walks in unbelief.
b. There is the **depressed believer** who feels rejected, unloved, inadequate, and worthless.
c. The **jealous person** is usually troubled with selfish sinful attitudes.
d. Some get **angry** when they believe that everything ought to go the way they wish. Research reveals that much anger is related to a *perceived* attack upon one's self.
e. Many emotional factors are involved in the sins that believers commit-some are highly emotionally motivated.

D. Present State of the World

World conditions have brought a profound impact toward the need for Pastoral counselling. There are so many sources of stress and emotional unrest that bring along a lot of pressure and emotional unrest; the following is a list of some of these *
Materialistic outlook of modern societies

- Our infatuation with self
- TV and the new morality
- The urbanization of society

- A ruthless society
- Competition in an open economy
- Working wives and mothers
- Religious apostasy
- Moral relativism has increased the incidence of sin and guilt
- Mankind becoming just a number in many instances
- A very transient population
- Pastors who abdicate their responsibility

Pastors have a God-given responsibility to teach, warn, rebuke and admonish the sheep of their flocks (Colossians 3:16; II Timothy 4: 2). The word, "admonition," or *nouthesia*, upon which Dr. Jay Adams bases his Nouthetic counselling, signifies "putting people in mind" of the truths they specifically need at a particular time.

Emotional and sinful distresses adversely affect one's worship, spiritual outlook, and Christian walk. The need for victory over sin and effectiveness in service and witness makes it imperative that the Pastor be involved when his people have problems. It would seem obligatory for Pastors to help their people avoid the dangers of walking "in the counsel of the ungodly" (Psalm 1:1).

Even though the secular psychologist may not openly seek to contradict or destroy the counsellee's faith in God, he still could do much harm to a believer and certainly would be at a handicap in dealing with the believer's problems. The Pastor, working with the person in a Biblical context, can achieve results which the secularist pyshcologist can never do.

II. THE COMMITMENT TO PASTORAL COUNSELLING:

A. The Pastor is endowed by God with more than empathy for people but with a burden to see them well. His burden is for the disturbed person, the perplexed person, the potential divorcee, those in financial bondage, the quarrelling church member, the aged, the rebellious youth, the newly married, and soon to be married, etc.

B. He is committed toward bringing change. Good counselling is communication between two or more people by which one person endeavours to effect change for one or more persons through the power of the Holy Spirit by the means of the Word of God. The task of the Christian counsellor is to call for repentance, which is a call for a change of mind leading to a change of life. The one who needs to repent may not be the counsellee but others with whom the counsellee lives or deals with daily, others whom the counsellor may never have a chance to meet.

Jay Adams writes, *"Counselling has to do with living. It has to do with how you evaluate and meet life situations. It has to do with how people live at home with other people and how they live with God. That's what counselling is all about– attitudes, values, beliefs, and behaviour."*

C. He is committed to Christian growth. Richard Gantz says, *"Biblical counselling is teaching people to live the Christian life."* It is assisting Christians in growth or progressive sanctification (Romans 8:29; II Corinthians 3:18; I John 3:2). The pastor must be committed to the task of counselling. He must comprehend the Biblical explanations for Christian growth, not only men's proposals, ideas, and methodology.

D. He will be committed regardless of the past. Tim LaHaye said, *"During the past 30 to 40 years western civilization has become increasingly obsessed with the idea that whenever a person becomes upset, he needs to see a secular, professional counsellor."* It was the liberal ministers who started a movement called "Clinical Pastoral Education" in America some 50 to 60 years ago.

In the past, conservative Bible believing Pastors were either too busy with evangelism and rebuilding ministries lost to the liberals, or they were overreacting to the point of believing that counselling was wrong because liberals and secularist were practicing it. And because the average Pastor did not feel prepared to counsel his people he would refer those in need to the secular psychologists. This was, and still is, a great error.

The lack of training and lack of a balanced ministry caused many Pastors to neglect the Divine call to minister to those in need (John 21). With the Bible school movement, there was an emphasis on evangelism to the loss of a balanced edification ministry. Also, there was a suspicion of higher education because of the liberals who were educated "out of" their adherence to the Bible. As a result many ministers did not receive a seminary education which could have given them the tools for an edification ministry among their own, that would include counselling.

CHAPTER FOUR

SOME GENERAL PRINCIPLES & PRACTICES IN NOUTHETIC COUNSELLING

I. THE MINISTRY OF COUNSELLING IN THE LOCAL CHURCH:

A. Calling people to remembrance.

B. Exhorting the people

C. Modeling Christ

D. Encouraging the people .

II. THE QUALITIES AND CHARACTERISTICS WE MUST HAVE:

It is as the shepherd, and not the psychiatrist, that God has assigned the task. The Holy Spirit with the Word of God will bring change in personality and character. The Bible is the textbook for counselling (II Peter 1:3) because it tells the believer how to relate to God and man. The following is a list of necessary qualities

A. We must possess knowledge.

B. We must have adaptability.

C. We must have genuine concern.

D. We need insight.

E. We must have "goodness, knowledge, wisdom" (Romans 15:14).

Since all Christians need counselling at some time in their lives, and all saints need to grow so they can counsel others, all of us must work at having the Biblical qualifications to counsel others.

1. *Goodness embraces both the involvement and the empathetic loving concern for the cousellee.* We love people because we are concerned for them. This should be a kind of spontaneous response to others in need. We are also to provoke others to love and to stimulate them to good works. (Hebrews 10:24.)

2. *We need knowledge, the understanding of the truths of the Word of God.* We must so saturate our lives with the principles of the Word of God that we can help meet the counselling needs of others. This involves adapting the Word of God to human situations without compromising it. We need the spiritual gift of discernment as well.

The counsellor will "exegete" the Word of God and thus apply the Scriptures in a practical fashion, by skilfully breaking it down in simple and applicable bits relevant to the counsellee's needs. He will labour to exalt Christ and meet human needs, and not just give verses like "pills."

If the Pastor-counsellor does not have the answer he will admit it, and search the Scriptures and wait on God's Revelation to discover the answer.

3. *The wisdom the Word of God gives is paramount.* Knowledge is not enough. We must know these books and chapters well: Proverbs chapters 1-8; Romans 6, 8, 12; Galatians 5, 6; Ephesians 4, 5, 6; Philippians 4; Colossians 3; James; I Peter 3; I John 1, 2, etc.)

The counsellor will have a humble confidence in the "thus saith the Lord" and will acknowledge that any benefit accruing from his counselling is ultimately attributable to the work of God.

The Pastoral counsellor will desire to lead the counsellee into the "will of God" for their life so that God might be glorified in their life. The counsellor will desire to—heal rather than hurt—build up rather than tear down—unite rather that divide and drive further away—bring about repentance rather than provoke to wrath.

F. We must instill "hope"

i. *The **need** of hope.* The counsellee often feels that all hope is gone. Life is meaningless when there is no hope. When meaning and purpose in life go so does the desire to live. I have often found that if hope is instilled, the counsellee begins to listen and desires to find Biblical answers to their problem(s). Hope to the troubled person is like a life raft to the drowning person.

ii. *How to instill hope.* This can come about <u>by speaking a kind word</u> for example, "I'm sincerely praying for you.", by sharing God's concern for them and showing them that God can meet their need. He is concerned, He cares for us, He made us and is aware of our every need. Hope is tremendously needed in their lives. Christ is touched with the feelings of our infirmities. There is nothing we could experience, but what He has also experienced. (Hebrews 4:14-16; 12:1-4; 13: 5, 6; I Peter 5:7; Psalm 55:22; I Corinthians 1:3-5)..

We instill hope <u>by personal testimony</u> of what God has done in our lives or the lives of others with whom we have laboured and who have been set free from the bondage of sin and failure. The restored counsellees can have tremendous impact by their testimony.

<u>Homework assignments</u> are given partly for the purpose of instilling hope toward change because they empower the counsellees when they can see that there are specific actions they can take to help themselves.

<u>As we reach out to them, sharing the hope of what God can and will do, can instil hope that becomes a bridge to their future</u>. In this, we must establish involvement (Acts 20:21) as we manifest compassion, empathy, feeling, and reaching out in Christ's Name to the needy person.

We must acknowledge that the person is not just a number. Strangers are simply friends we are yet to make . We must be willing to show emotion and yet be careful that we are not too intimately involved. Showing discretion, and yet being compassionate, is very important; Christ had tears.

In one sense each person needs at least one other person; no man is an island and we must convince the counsellee that he is someone who is loved. There is a degree of professionalism that must be maintained, and yet we contend that every person is a friend.

G. We must receive talk of personal failure seriously and calmly.

1. *Don't act surprised*. If the counsellee says he is worthless, don't act surprised, or if he tells some sordid, immoral story or of some involvement, don't be shocked or show dismay, etc.

2. *The counsellee may have failed.* Often the person is experiencing great amounts of guilt because in many instances he is simply guilty. Don't minimize his guilt, he will only feel more guilty. And to minimize his problem is to minimize his story and show disinterest toward the seriousness of what he is saying.

3. *Take him at his word.* But also realize that this is probably not the total story. Often only the symptoms are being shared and the root problems are still buried or hidden. You must get to the real problem since it may be hidden behind the presented problem.

H. We must give authoritative instruction.

1. *Christian, Biblical counselling involves authoritative instruction, both in content and in loving attitude on the part of the counsellor.* (Proverbs 2:1-4, 8; 2:5-15; 1:8; 3:1, 4; 6:20-23.) We must use the Word of God in an authoritative manner as Solomon in the book of Proverbs gave authoritative instruction.

2. *Focus upon Scriptural living.* Love will blossom as counsellors focus their attention upon purification of the heart, cleansing of the conscience, and building of genuine trust. The trust must be toward God, His Word, and toward the counsellor.

I. We must be a good listener.

1. *Don't interrupt! Hear them out* (Proverbs 18:13; James 1:19).

2. *Listen with the ears.* Don't gaze elsewhere or arrange the desk, etc. Interrupt only if necessary.

3. *Listen for feelings, facts, overtones, undertones, hidden meanings.* Listen selectively (relative to needs), listen responsively, empathetically, not proposing a solution until you have understood the problem. Don't be involved in planning a reply.

J. We must rely on the power of God.

1. *Rely on the working of the Holy Spirit and the power of God* through you and through the Word of God. Don't just give "lip service" to

this, but expect God to be at work in the counselling session. Anticipate God being at work in the life of the counsellee and be watching for it by faith (Hebrews 11:1, 6). Walk with the Holy Spirit.

2. *Begin and close every session with prayer.* Let them know that you are praying for them (Proverbs 2:6, 7; 3:5, 6; James 1:5). And really do pray for them in earnest, fervent supplication (Ephesians 6:18).

K. We must give advice carefully, prayerfully, not hastily.

1. It is easy to think that we must always have a quick answer for everything and that we always ought to have an answer.

2. Don't be afraid to tell the person that you need to pray about a certain problem and give it more study.

3. It is better to say nothing than to say the wrong thing.

4. Constantly check your advice with the Word of God. It should be your primary source book at all times. Memorizing and meditating on the Word of God will help prepare you for times of need.

III. THE CHANGE THAT COMES THROUGH LOVE AND FORGIVENESS:

A. Love is the goal and the paramount need.

(John 15: 9, 12, 17; I Timothy 1:5). Twelve times God says in His word "Love one another."

1. Love for God and love for one's neighbour constitute the sum of God's requirements for the Christian.
2. Love is the ultimate answer to all the problems of living that the Christian counsellor deals with (I John 4:17, 18).
3. A primary principle of Biblical counselling is this: As a person moves closer to God *through His love-* which includes both mercy and truth expressed through His Word and through His Holy Spirit-he will change in the areas of thoughts, emotions and actions.
4. God's love can touch a person's spirit, and one consistent result of a deepened spiritual life is an improved mental-emotional-behavioural life. *The change occurs through love, not through psychological techniques and training.*
5. Only God's love can **transform** a life. God's love is infinitely more intense than human love. God's love is a powerful, consistent, and dependable force that, when received, transforms the individual and enables him to walk by faith, to hope in God, and to love God and others according to the Great Commandment (Deuteronomy 6:5; Leviticus 19:18; Matthew 22:36-40).
6. As one reads about how Jesus ministered to each individual, one learns to depend upon God to lead and one learns God's way of **ministering truth in LOVE** and in power. Paul prayed for the Ephesians that they would know the love of God in their daily life (Ephesians 3:16-20; 4:2; 5: 1, 2, 25, 29, 31).

7. In life there is either the manifestation of self-love or of God's love. Does the counsellee understand the basis of God's love? Does he understand the demonstration of God's love through the cross? Does he respond to God's love? Does he love God and others? Is he preoccupied with self? Does he walk in self-love and self-will? Does he manifest submission or rebellion?
8. God's love is the primary motivation for growth and change. Receiving God's love and following the "great commandment" of Matthew 22:36 are major goals in Biblical counseling, (I John 4).

In teaching the love of God the counsellor will stress those aspects of God's character that the counsellee needs to hear, such as

- God's love undergirds, amplifies, and modifies every quality of His character.
- His sovereignty, power, truth, holiness, faithfulness, wisdom, justice, righteousness, grace, mercy, forgiveness, patience, and tenderness, etc.
- The counsellee needs to know, believe and receive the love of God. He will need to understand that this is ours NOT by merit or works, but totally of grace. And that God's love is manifested even in the difficult things, for everything comes through His Hand of love. (Rom. 8:28, 29.)

- Some equate love with having their own way, which is another form of self-love, and making self as god. God's love flows to us from the Cross, which is a vivid picture of self-abasement for our sakes (Heb. 12:1-4).

B. Receiving Forgiveness is also a Paramount Need.

1. Forgiveness provides freedom from guilt and enables a person to walk in right relationship with God and man. It is the means for restoring a relationship that has been clouded with sin. Forgiveness is one of the essential considerations in counselling. So often people find it difficult to truly forgive and the problems continue because of its lack; (Psalms. 32:5; Eph. 4: 32; Colossian. 3:12-14).

2. The only way there can be true healing and restoration is by repentance. There can be the joy of full forgiveness through confession. Psalms 32 and 51 would be very important for the counsellee to study. God wants each one of us to know forgiveness and restoration with the burden of sin completely lifted. The counsellee must also be led to forgive others.

3. The study of Luke 15 shows God's heart. He forgives, receives us back, and withholds condemnation even though we deserve nothing. Many of the saved are trapped in self-condemnation. It becomes a habit of thinking and responding to self as perhaps they have been thinking and responding to others—with criticism.

4. When a person does not confess to God, repent, and believe God's forgiveness, he falls prey to self-condemnation. Self-condemnation is a dangerous activity of pride, it is a result of the 'self' playing the role of God. When self plays god, he condemns, punishes, rewards, and excuses himself for behaviour, depending upon whether he is a strict god (perfectionist) or a lenient god who tends to pamper and excuse self. God wants to be GOD in every area of our lives including the areas of judgment and mercy. He has the standard of behaviour and He is the One who grants pardon. We need to live by His Standard and not ours.

5. We need to discern right and wrong, but leave all judgment to God alone, lest we fall into both self-condemnation and into criticism of others as well. When God forgives us, the matter is finished, signed, sealed, guaranteed, and forgotten. Therefore, when we confess sin, we must also accept the truth of His forgiveness (Psalms 103: 3, 8-14; Isaiah 44: 22; I John 1:7-2:2).

6. Has the counsellee truly and fully repented? Has the person accepted God's forgiveness? Does the counsellee practice self-condemnation?

- Verbal confession strengthens the one who may doubt that he can be forgiven and gives him the opportunity to seal the confession and repentance through the prayer time with the counsellor.

- A Biblical counsellor is quick to promote confession and repentance, and to help the person accept God's forgiveness (James 5:19, 20).
- The counsellor will want to help the counsellee to begin to respond to God's love in faith, responsibility and submission.

C. Forgiving Others Is Imperative.

Many people live under condemnation and guilt because they have refused to forgive others (Matthew 6:14, 15). The choice to forgive activates the work of the Holy Spirit in a person's life.

1. Forgiveness places trust in God to deal with both the offender and the results of the offence. God only has the right to avenge, (bring revenge) in the event of the wrongdoing.
2. Forgiveness releases both the forgiver and the forgiven from a relationship of blame, retaliation, bitterness, and resentment. The choice to forgive releases the flow of God's love through the forgiving one.
3. The counsellee who finds it difficult to forgive must be helped to move away from a feeling-oriented life. He must learn to readily apply Biblical principles and commands toward forgiveness (Ephesians 4:32, 5:1, 2; Colossians 3:12-14).

The counsellor might desire to outline the following steps for the counsellee to help him toward forgiveness:

- Tell God about the situation, confess sins, and ask God to bring healing, forgiveness and the ability to forgive (Ephesians 4:32; Ps. 32:5).
- Choose to forgive and not to hold the offence against the offender.
- Consider the greatness of the forgiveness of God and the great cost of our forgiveness made available through Christ's death on the cross (Romans 5:8; Ephesians 1:7; Colossians 1:14; Revelation 1:4, 5).
- If you have sinned against the offender, go to him and confess your sin and ask forgiveness without casting blame or even expecting him to ask forgiveness of you (Colossians 3:10-14).
- Maintain the attitude of forgiveness and resist the temptation to nurse past wounds.
- Actively do good toward those who have sinned against you, and labour to love them (Matthew 5: 43, 44).
- If the unforgiving attitudes and bitterness recur because of reminders of the offence, or because of the offence repeated, maintain the choice to forgive. There must be the "will" to forgive even if the feelings are slow to catch up.

CHAPTER FIVE

FORMING, AND ADOPTING A NOUTHETIC COUNSELLING MODEL

From observations during training and practice, I think that people are motivated by **three** basic dynamics or controlling factors in their lives. There are <u>those who basically are</u>

1. **behaviourally motivated.**
2. For most people their thought life, (**beliefs and unbeliefs**) is the controlling dynamic which brings about the resultant behaviour. (I believe that the greater number of people is found in this grouping.) Still others are
3. **motivated predominantly by their emotions** as they react emotionally and then think about their sinful behaviour later.

It is my intention to set forth counselling models based to some extent on these three dynamics or controlling factors which seemingly motivate people whom we counsel.

PHYSICAL ASPECTS INVOLVED

As part of the thorough preparation for the counselling session the counsellor must consider whether there could be physical contributing factors in the life of the counsellee. You will need to know if the counsellee is taking any form of medication etc.

An essential component of the holistic assessment form is to have a questionnaire designed to uncover potential problems in this area. The person may be adversely affected by medications that could greatly influence their attitudes, conduct, etc. So this must be taken into consideration.

SUPPORT NETWORK—FAMILY, FRIENDS, CHURCH.

As you work with the counsellees you may find it necessary to work out a support team for their ongoing counselling. If the person is having problems with alcohol, drugs, or having difficulty with a sinful life-style of whatever kind, he may need to be helped with constant oversight. Some churches have families who are willing to give this kind of support or ongoing aid to a person or family who must have constant oversight. This may need to continue until they are set free from the problem, and during all the time they are in extensive counselling. This kind of help can be indispensable.

EMOTIONAL FACTOR—DEPRESSION, ANGER, BITTERNESS, ETC.

Many who will come to us are distraught and overcome by emotional factors which seem to dominate their lives moment by moment. The Word of God speaks much to these sinful life patterns which are manifested in thought life, in emotional responses, and in actions.

Some people are emotionally controlled in many ways. They may be anxious, fretful, worrying-type people. Very often, because of pride, the person is controlled by his feelings. The predominant reaction may be manifested in angry outbursts, bitterness, holding grudges, and unforgiving attitudes.

These sinful life-style patterns do not "stand by themselves," but generally are brought about by what we have done about our past PROGRAMMING AND PRESENT EVENTS or CIRCUMSTANCES. In SINFUL SELF-TALK (or personal conversational evaluations) we are considering those events and past programming which God has allowed and the programming the persons have built into their own lives. This is clearly seen in such Biblical stories as Joseph's life, Elijah's life, and the children of Israel's experience in journey from Egypt, etc.

Many people think that they cannot control their emotional responses and those emotions or feelings cause their behaviour and therefore, they are not accountable for their actions.

The counsellee will never change the sinful emotional responses until he calls sin –sin, and sees the source as found in his own sinful, self-talk evaluation. The sinful self-talk is usually manifested in unbelief and the embracing of lies which have been rehearsed mentally over and over again. Emotions are not usually the causes, but the results, of thoughts.

- Erroneous thinking and related feelings often gets a person into deep misery and complicated conflicts.
- One of the primary concerns of a Biblical counsellor is truth itself. He will watch for error or distortion in the counsellee's thinking, words and feelings.
- A Biblical counsellor will attempt to help the person recognize wrong feelings and the result of submitting to those feelings.
- The counsellor will encourage the counsellee to accept and believe what God has said over and above his feelings. Because feelings are deep and they are usually very close to the very heart of man, they appear difficult to change but God can bring change by the renewing of the mind (Romans 12:2).
- Emotions or feelings may range from the sublime to the sinful. When feelings and desires agree with the Word of God and the indwelling Holy Spirit they are beautiful and even holy (Galatians 5:22, 23; 5:15-17.).
- When emotions and desires originate in the flesh, they become focused on self and grieve the Holy Spirit. The counsellor will want to be sure that the counsellee does not deny the existence of feelings and desires.
- The counsellee's feelings or emotions are formed by his natural environment, circumstances, past experiences, patterns or

habits of life and by his perception of these factors.
- Because of hurts and distortions of perception, feelings are often unreliable indicators of truth. Certain feelings may be just the opposite of what is true.
- The counsellee can change emotional responses by "putting on Christ" and being renewed daily by the Word of God (Romans 13:14; Ephesians 4:23).

A. Dealing with Anger and Hurts.

1. The single greatest force to change a person's emotional response in sinful ways is the power of the love of God.

2. God's "perfect love" casts out fear, heals personal hurts, replaces wrong anger and changes rejection to acceptance (I John 4:17-19).

3. Hurt and anger often need to be dealt with in counselling. These basic sinful responses to situations in life can be broken as habits of reaction. God's method is clearly given in Ephesians 4:22-24. These responses can become strongholds of sin from which the counsellee can and must be set free (Romans 6: 6-14).

4. Emotions are related to thinking. Knowing and acting according to the Word of God will enable the individual to overcome explosive and internally prolonged anger which may lead to wrath, bitterness, and depression. It is changed

thinking that will greatly help those who have problems with anger, hurt, and bitterness.
5. Thinking influences emotions. Emotions are not independent. They have been nursed, expressed, and encouraged to remain by thinking the kind of thoughts that will prolong them.

B. The Problem of Fears.

1. Fear as an emotion manifests itself in many debilitating ways and prevents rational responses to life's situations and problems.
2. Fear never comes from God (II Timothy 1:7). While there is a wholesome fear that keeps us from danger, or accident and a "fear of the Lord" which is good, much fear stems from unbelief and doubt.
3. A person can overcome fleshly fear by drawing close to God, remembering His caring nature and His power to keep us (Psalm 27:1, 14). The counsellor must develop a faith walk and be able to teach the counsellee how to walk by faith and in sweet submission. The living words of the Bible are given to enable us to overcome the feelings of fear and dread (Isaiah 41:10; 40:28-31).

C. The Emotion of Rejection.

1. Rejection is a common emotional response seen in the lives of many with whom we may counsel.
2. A feeling of rejection often includes loneliness, self-pity, rebellion, depression and even suicide.

3. Everyone experiences rejection at some point in life, and to some degree. It may be real or just perceived.
4. Those who have a pattern of rejection may respond in one of the following ways—try to gain acceptance through performance, retreat from others to prevent further rejection, or they may become very hard and indifferent.
5. God's remedy for rejection is truth. The truth of His love, our position in Christ, and all that we have in Him should set the person free from the feelings of rejection, IF those things are accepted and applied to their life. (See Ephesians 1:1-12; I Corinthians 6: 9-11.)
6. Only Divine Love can heal the deep wounds of rejection.

DIRECTIVE COUNSELLING– BEHAVIOUR AS THE BASIC MOTIVATING DYNAMIC.

We should not rule out beliefs or attitudes as dynamics which affect people. Behavioural change comes about largely by getting the person to directly confront and, persistently work on actions as the source of the problems. Therefore, great importance is placed upon the "put off and put on" dynamic which is so clearly set forth in the Word of God.

We have stated that nouthetic counselling is Biblical counselling which is directive and confrontational. It consists of verbal counselling in which behaviour, attitudes and beliefs are changed. This is the whole process of counselling.

I. THE ACTIVITY IN DIRECTIVE COUNSELLING.

A. Judging activity, not motives, of the person's actions. We are to teach or set forth the norms of faith and practice (John 7:24).

B. Convicting activity. This is a ministry of reproving the person who is not aware of his sin or is still unrepentant. Conviction of sin comes when the Holy Spirit uses the Word of God shared by the counsellor and studied by the counsellee (Hebrews 4:12).

C. Changing activity, which means to set straight again. This consists of breaking harmful, sinful habits and seeking to overcome failures and weaknesses. This includes reconciliation, restitution, and putting on new patterns of behaviour and living (Colossians 3:8-14).

D. Structuring activity is also needed, wherein there is structuring or training in righteousness. This involves laying out a personal Biblical pattern of living for the counsellee to replace the unbiblical one.

II. THE NATURE OF DIRECTIVE COUNSELLING.

A. Authoritative—because the Word of God is authoritative.

B. Assertive—The counsellor should assert Biblical principles and not use questions as a habit or as a softening technique in the presentation of truth. One cannot have a true discussion (or dialogue) of the "Thus saith the Lord."

C. Confrontative—it affords a personal face-to-face involvement that refuses to avoid the often unpleasant but necessary task of assisting a person who has a problem.

D. Flexible and Adaptable—The Christian counsellor will study the Word of God and be as flexible as the Scriptures. He will not approach problems from preconceived notions of what is wrong and what to do. The Biblical counsellor adapts his Biblical principles of counselling to changing and unpredictable circumstances. He has order and structure to his approach, but is willing to bend his schedule for the good of the counsellee. His agenda will fit the need of the person and will work out agreements when there are differing ideas.

E. Non-manipulative- Biblical counsellors do not manipulate and control others. They prayerfully analyze the believer's problem according to Scriptural categories and truth and then point them to God's solutions. They will exhort, encourage, warn, persuade, and use rewards also when helpful. God's Word becomes the motivation, and love for God the controlling factor, and not control of the counsellee or counsellor.

F. Godly accurate language– The counsellor will help the counsellee to relate his language to reality. (Here we see the cognitive aspects.) Exaggerations and generalities should be examined for what they are and what they are to convey. The counsellor will stop and correct crude and vulgar words.

III. PROCEDURE OF DIRECTIVE COUNSELLING.

A. Steps toward Counselling Interview.

1. Make the appointment- your time is valuable. Explain the importance of attending the counseling sessions and that in some cases it may require sacrificing their time in much in the same way as they would in in getting to their medical doctor.
2. Gather the data to diagnose the problem. This may necessitate getting data over a number of sessions. Use a holistic assessment form. Sometimes other forms may be required for this.
3. Arrive at a Biblical diagnosis and present that diagnosis to the counsellee. If a sin problem is apparent the counsellee should be encouraged to repent of that sin to all who are involved.
4. The counsellee should agree to a programme of dehabituation and rehabituation if needed.
5. There must be homework assignments between sessions for the practice of the new patterns to be implemented in the life.
6. As time progresses and needs are being met, you can set an approximate termination time.

B. Charting the Dehabituation and Rehabituation Process.

- *Building patterns for a walk in righteous.*
- *A breaking of persistent patterns of sin.*

- *A process leading to change and a process of change.*

This may take between 8—12 weeks of counselling or even more, depending on the seriousness of the problem (s).

IV. BRINGING ABOUT BIBLICAL CHANGE IN DIRECTIVE COUNSELLING.

A. Change is the Goal in all Biblical Counselling.

   1. We all know and agree that change is difficult. (Going to bed early, getting up early, overcoming anger, scheduling our time, controlling one's temper, stopping smoking, losing weight, starting new habits– all these things and many more are not easy for some.)
   2. Eliminating the problem is not the goal of counselling. Helping the person to personal happiness is not the goal of counselling. Change that results in conformity to the image of Jesus Christ is the goal.
   3. Failing, floundering is the daily occurrence with most counsellees. Most counsellees are either unwilling or do not know how to make the change that God requires of them. *Learned behaviour is often confused with inherited nature.*

B. Changing the Past is not the Goal Either.

   1. We need to forget the past, and not attempt to change it (Philippians 3:13, 14). (The past can only be dealt with in the present by forgiveness, rectification, reconciliation and other changes that must be made today.)

2. It is the counsellee who needs to be changed, and not his past. We can only deal with the guilt that is involved in the past. Help him to know and thank God for forgiveness and then to reach out to that which is ahead.

   3. He can be assured a better future by making behaviour and personality changes in the present.

   Many counsellees do not enjoy abundant living in the present because of past sins. They worry, fret, toss and turn, but the past is the past and often times, robs a person of joy and victory in the present.

   4. We must call for repentance. The task of the Biblical counsellor is to call for repentance—a change of mind and will leading to a change of life. True repentance is something that the Holy Spirit always brings about in true change. (II Corinthians 7:10).

C. There must be a Changing of Present Patterns from the Past.

   1. The past is present with the counsellee most plainly in his personality, attitudes and life-style. (We do need to understand many aspects of the past so that we can help them bring change.)

   2. We do not see change that sticks because of the repetition of sin that becomes habitual. There is also the repetitive, habitual pattern of sin, confession and forgiveness and then back into the cycle again.

It takes *discipline* to bring about behavioural and personality change. The Scriptures give the needed direction, hope and goals– the Holy Spirit provides the power—but Godly discipline is the method. The person without discipline is like a city without walls (Proverbs 25:26, 28).

One's personality and behaviour traits may become so much a part of him that at times a counsellor may confuse it with hereditary traits. That is why we must have a thorough, positive, working knowledge of the Word of God. Most attempts at changing are like New Year's resolutions–they are ineffective. It is not enough to confess the sin. Counsellees must receive help to begin the change, or discouragement and continued failure will bring hopelessness.

D. Dehabituation and Rehabituation Will Effect Change

1. God calls for change in the manner of life. "Put off and Put on" (Ephesians 4: 22-24; Colossians 3: 5-14).
2. God does not call for a cessation but for a change. Change must accompany cessation. Change is a two-faceted process and both must be present for results. (This two-part process is found often in the Word of God.)
3. Change is directed toward a way of life, not just some activities that are involved in such living. The counsellee is renewed unto a change of his whole life style.

E. There must be a Breaking and a Making of Habits.

1. A manner of life is a habitual way of living, for we are creatures of habit. Many habits have become second nature.

2. Discipline is the key– (Note I Timothy 4:7– "exercise"). This is the word gymnazo or gymnastics—to work out. This is the "key" to victory for the Christian counsellee. (II Peter 2:14; Hebrews 5:14)

We become Godly or ungodly by the exercise or the practice of right or wrong. Counsellors must help the counsellee to break loose from the web of sin, the habit of sin, and help him replace the wrong habits with Christ-like habits and Christ-like ways.

- Habits work for us or against us. The counsellor must continually reckon with habits problems.
- The Biblical way to Godliness is not easy or simple, but it is the solid and true way.
- Negative attitudes can be changed, tempers can be controlled, but it takes discipline and proper motivation.
- The Christian life is a life of continual change. The life of the saved is called a "walk" and not a rest (Ephesians 4, 5; II Corinthians 3:18).
- Counsellors must recognize that some counsellees give up too soon.

- Change is a grace-motivated effort, not the work of the flesh. Liberty comes through the discipline of the Word of God, not apart from it.
- It is prayerful obedience to the Scriptures that produces Godly patterns.
- Counsellees are happiest when they are living within the framework of God's Word.
- One's "**feelings**" are perhaps the biggest problem of all. We must live according to the Word of God regardless of how we may feel.
- It is not enough to put off one way of life; new habits of the new way of life must be put in place of the old.
- It is not enough to just go to church, pray, and read the Bible. There must be more than that to draw from in the counsellees' repertoire. It takes effort -literally "being exercised" unto Godliness, to change.

V. BASIC ELEMENTS INVOLVED IN BIBLICAL CHANGE.

A. Becoming Aware of the Practice of Habits.

1. A habit is a "behaviour pattern" established by frequent repetition that reveals itself by constant performance. It may be consciously or unconsciously acquired.

2. "Habit simplifies the movements required to achieve a given result, makes them more accurate and diminishes fatigue."

In many people, by the age of thirty, the character has set like plaster, and change is not easy. As early as possible in life, the right kind of actions must become automatic and habitual. In the acquisition of a new habit, or the leaving of an old one, we must take care to launch ourselves with the strongest and most decided initiative possible. Never suffer an exception to occur until the new habit is securely rooted in the life. New habits take about three to five weeks to cement into the life.

The person must seize the very first possible opportunity to act on every resolution made, and on every emotional prompting in the direction of the habit he aspires to be gained.

B. Understanding the Dynamics of Habitual Practices.

1. Very quickly the individual feels comfortable while performing the habit.
2. He responds without thinking of certain stimuli or given situations in a habitual way. This is gained from birth onward.
3. The counsellee engages in the practice of the habit (or at least may begin to do so without conscious thought or decision.

C. Becoming Aware of the Occasion of the Practice of the Habit.

1. The person must become aware of the <u>nature</u>, the <u>frequency</u>, and the <u>occasion</u> of any practice or habit. Habits do not stand alone; usually they are related to something else. The person who "*blows up*" may be doing so because they are triggered by jealousy.

2. What is the person doing? Why are they doing it? What is the habit? Unless the person is aware of what they are doing and why, they will not know how to correct the problem or practice. (What is it associated with, or linked to, and what possibly triggers the practice?)

D. Discovering the Biblical Alternative.

1. What is the proper practice, pattern or habit to replace every improper one?

2. Notice the many portions of Scripture which bring together the necessity of putting off and putting on, or where the opposites are set forth for us to see (James 5:12; Ephesians 4:17-32; Colossians 3:8-14.)

E. Working at Bringing Motivation into the Scene.

1. A willingness to change is needed; without a desire, it is l unlikely that it will happen. Godly sorrow works repentance (II Corinthians 7:10).

2. All motivation must be based upon the Word of God. If it is not Scriptural it will not last. The Word should be used properly as the best motivation (II Corinthians 5:11, 14).

- Help the person see their position in Christ Jesus (Ephesians 1:3-12).
- Help them see what Christ desires of them (II Peter 1:3-12).
- Help them through a consequence /reward system that will give them the impetus to change. (Malachi 3:9-13; Deuteronomy 11:18-25.)

F. Helping Them Structure Things toward Change.

1. **Structuring** is very important because it sets the stage for change.
2. Every Christian has a **battle** between the old nature and the new nature, and this naturally brings inward conflict. The flesh has sinful, often very wicked, desires.
3. The counsellees' activities, surroundings, and associations should be consistent with and aid their avowed desire to put off a sinful practice (Romans 13:14). Every **counsellee has lust within their members**.
4. Structure facilitates change as the counsellee puts himself into a new environment to bring change.
5. One must rearrange his environment, schedules, activities, etc., to become facilitators rather than impediments to change.
6. The person must do what God desires him to do. There is a personal responsibility toward Godliness which must be satisfied.

G. We Must Help the Person "Break the Links" in the chain of sin.

1. We must help them trace the problem back to its origin and stop the problem at its outset.

   This may also necessitate understanding the programming—sinful self-talk practices, attitudes, emotions, and finally the behavioural aspects. This may mean we will need to understand much of their past which has led to their viewpoints, habitual sinful practices, etc.

2. Chaining is a proven learning theory as well as a Biblical concept. It asserts that by manipulating the various components in the chain of sin you can prevent the final behaviour from occurring.

   Many counsellors and counsellees think of change only in terms of changing the full-blown **problem**. It is important to break the problem down into all of its component parts. The failure to work out our problems daily will bring frustration—and the person will probably "blow up" or become very depressed.
3. To break the chain of sin requires ability to stop an action. This could take place at the point of **resistance** or at a point of **restraint.**

Resistance is the God-given ability that makes it possible for the person to delay his responses. We are not animals that live by reflex only. We do have brains that enable us to resist and reject a sinful course of action. When we do not practice such rejection it is probably because we would rather enjoy the sinful action, thought, etc., or we just did not work at catching ourselves in the sinful practice.

The goal is Biblical "action" not sinful "reaction." We are to be controlled by the Scriptures and not by the situation. Breaking the destructive patterns that "accelerate sin" involves the structuring and development of new responses. Resistance is to work at preventing the practice.

Example: Instead of screaming, the mother works at developing the habit of speaking softly. (Proverbs 15:1; 16:32; 29: 11, 20; 30:33.)

Restraint *is to work at curtailing the problem.* Restraint is the approach when the resistance fails. It is stopping oneself prior to going too far in sinful responses or habitual action. Restraint is the "recognition of sin" and seeking immediate forgiveness for it and obtaining help to discontinue the sin. **It is thought before action or speech as the element in the restraint of evil.** Memorization and meditation on the Word of God are very helpful in all of this effort toward change.

H. Aiding in the Practice of New Patterns.

It is very important to help the counsellees discipline themselves in order to have the "key" to holiness. There is no option for Godliness as the goal of the Christian life. One's whole life must be disciplined, set up, organized and running day-by-day toward the goal of Christ-like living. It will necessitate sacrifice; there are no shortcuts.

VI. GETTING HELP FROM OTHERS FOR BIBLICAL CHANGE.

Change is difficult because without thinking we respond to temper, we clam up, and internalize resentment, etc. and we live according to the sinful patterns and habits that we have developed over the years.

Others can aid in building new habits and the breaking of the sinful practices. This takes willingness and an understanding that it is a process. The Scriptures continually stress the need for "mutual help." (Romans 15:1; Galatians 6:2.)

People do not seek help for many reasons. Pride is one of the primary reasons (I Corinthians 10:12; Proverbs 16:18). Because people are spiritually unwise they do not see the need for the counsel they desperately need. They hate to admit they have failed and cannot make it on their own and therefore need assistance.

When people fight over things like squeezing the toothpaste tube in the middle, turning lights off, etc., they give evidence of a number of things that require change:

- Their problem is much bigger than the issue (or issues) over which they are currently quarreling.
- They are not seeking solutions to problems; they are concerned about making points, proving themselves to be right, and the other person wrong.
- When there are flaming emotions over little issues it is because there are weightier issues that have not settled. From those confrontations they have emotional hurts which affect their daily responses.
- People do not look for solutions to personal conflicts until they have responded in repentance of their sins.

VII. WE MUST STRESS THEIR WHOLE RELATIONSHIP TO CHRIST.

(The Whole Life is Important for Change.)

A. <u>All must be Discussed when Extended Counselling is done</u>.
- Devotions
- Church attendance
- Witnessing as a vital part of growth and victory
- Repentance, confession, and reconciliation, etc.

B. <u>The Goal is not to Make People Better, or Happier.</u>

You will want to focus not just on their immediate problem but also on their relationship to Christ. Get them into a Bible study; help them know their position in HIM.

VIII. HELPING THEM HANDLE LIFE'S DOMINATING PROBLEMS:

Don't focus on the life dominating problem only; consider the total person and focus on the patterns which make up the life as well. Total restructuring must take place and this means dealing with the problem as it relates to all areas of the life.

Dominating problems are those problems that affect every area of one's life—drugs, alcoholism, homosexuality, etc.

Every area of the person's life must come under review. A drunkard, for example, develops sinful patterns of family relations, irresponsibility toward job, church, neighbours, finances, pressure, etc. He has difficulty dealing with his many problems as well as the major sin problem.

COGNITIVE ASPECTS OF NOUTHETIC COUNSELLING—RECOGNITION OF THOUGHTS AND THEIR EFFECT ON THE LIFE.

Nouthetic counselling always includes dealing with both the inner man and the outer man- with thoughts and emotions and with words and actions. For a Christian to live a consistent life, his thoughts, emotions, words, and actions must cooperate with the indwelling Holy Spirit.

Christ emphasized the relationship of inner thoughts, understanding, and desire, with outer actions and words (Matthew 12: 34-35). In the psychological world there is an argument between those counsellors who deal with behaviour and those who deal with thought. As far as the Bible is concerned both are important. Proverbs 16:3 says "Commit thy works unto the Lord, and thy thoughts shall be established." In Romans 10:9, 10 we see the combination of belief or thinking and action or confession; there is an internal choice of belief combined with an external action of confession.

What a person does influences his thoughts and what a person thinks influences what he does. Sinful thoughts can eventually lead to sinful behaviour. Conversely, thoughts often conform to behaviour. People may distort Scripture to fit their behaviour. In Scriptural counselling inner thoughts and outer works are intertwined. The outer renewal consists of new ways of behaving that are consistent with Biblical principles.

But to make this work there must also be a change in the thinking of the person. Change must take place both in the inner life (thoughts) as well as the outer life (or the actions). The problems of lust and pride, for example, must be faced basically, first, as thoughts, as well as the outcome produced in sinful practices or actions. (John 8:31-32; Proverbs 23:7.) Abiding in God's Word means more than casual believing; abiding implies thinking, feeling, and acting according to faith in His Word.

God expects change in thinking. This take place when the Christian chooses to be transformed by the renewing of the mind by the Word of God (Ephesians 4:23; Romans 12:2; Colossians 3: 8-14).

God desires to set us free from sinful practices. Wrong **thinking** causes havoc in emotions and error in actions. When a person's thoughts, feelings, and actions are based on the Bible, he receives wisdom, peace, righteousness, and the blessed fruit of the Spirit.

God desires accurate, truthful thinking. Erroneous thinking often gets a person into deep misery and complicated conflicts (Ephesians 4:15, 25).

1. Therefore, one of the primary concerns ought to be that we walk in truth.
2. The counsellor must be greatly concerned about the thought life of the counsellee (John 8:31, 32).
3. We must help the person to focus on what is right to think (Philippians 4:8).
4. As thought life changes, behaviour will change. Accurate thinking will free a counsellee from the bondage of sin, Satan's lies, and the practice of self-deception or telling oneself lies that are embraced and practiced.
5. Lies are often in the form of generalizations.
6. Thoughts can be continuously evil. Sinful imaginations and falsehoods can form strongholds in the mind and then in the will (II Corinthians 10:3-5).
7. The mind is a battleground on which thoughts from the world, the flesh, and the devil can vie against the truth of God.
8. Imaginations can include fears, doubts, and other forms of unbelief -belief which can undermine the Christian's walk.

I. RECOGNITION OF THE IMPORTANCE OF ONE'S THOUGHTS.

A. People's thinking includes their beliefs, attitudes, opinions and values.

1. Thoughts take the form of internalized sentences or self-talk. In fact, it is said that we can internalize thoughts in speed upwards to 1300 words a minute.

2. People are constantly telling themselves various sane or crazy things that are reflected in their emotions and actions.
3. People can live the most fulfilling, creative, and emotionally satisfying lives by disciplining their thinking so that it is God honouring.

B. Thinking is a train of ideas manifesting itself in sub-vocal speech.

We can alter our emotions by altering our words. We normally react logically to our own words. For example, you will feel differently if you-

1. Call a person careless instead of calling him a stupid idiot.
2. Call a person black instead of calling him a nigger.
3. Call a person a strong leader instead of calling him a dictator.
4. You say the boss saw you make a mistake and brought it to your attention instead of, "My boss chewed me out."

Our inner thoughts or words spoken to ourselves do have a great influence upon our emotions and our actions. Irrational (sinful) thinking produces disaster in the emotional sphere. A good example of this is the person who carries much free-floating anger around with him and who, as a result, also finds the world he encounters to be an angry one in order to justify his own feelings of anger. In this case, where emotions have influenced thinking, it is evident that it is the thinking element in the original free-floating hostility that needs to be discovered and handled if the person is to live more effectively.

C. Not only our perceptions but our evaluation of what we perceive causes our emotions and our reactions.

1. We perceive our own thoughts and memories, and evaluate them as well. Emotions do not exist mysteriously in their own right; they are caused. Emotions usually are not causes; but they are like the smoke detector—they only tell us that something is wrong.

2. We can have emotional reactions to thoughts by our evaluative self-talk, and out of that we can produce many sinful responses that can be sorrowful for many. Emotion, then, is almost always caused and controlled by thinking.

3. People do not go to counsellors (or psychiatrists) primarily because their thoughts are irrational but because they are hurting emotionally, even though they do have thoughts that are sinful and irrational, since they are not founded on truth.

4. It is human (sinful) nature to pervert and distort truth (Jeremiah 17:9). When one makes a study of what God says about the sinful, wicked, unregenerated mind, it is obvious that man's thoughts will be sinful and distorted, bringing many hurtful results.

5. We do most of our important thinking in terms of self-talk or internalized sentences. The Biblical counsellor will work with the counsellee to help him see the need to substitute self-defeating lies with Biblical truths that h bring misery. Understanding the source of emotions is to understand that they are composed of:-

  i. our perception;
  ii. our evaluating thoughts; and
  iii. our emotive feelings.

It must be noted that the evaluations that the brain automatically makes are positive, negative, or relatively neutral. Emotions, then, are value judgments and they are always logical, correct, and appropriate to **how you are evaluating a situation.** This is why when the Word of God is memorized and meditated upon daily it will greatly affect one's emotions, and consequently the actions or pattern of behaviour.

The counsellor must encourage people to **question** the validity of their sincerely held beliefs, attitudes and thoughts. His aim is also to help them make rational, Biblical choices.

Our brains often control us by habits to which we have become enslaved. Habits are formed by our repeatedly choosing to do something. **For example,** when you habitually think the same types of thoughts about your perception of a particular extreme event, you will begin to automatically react to that type of perception with positive, negative, or neutral feelings. <u>Your emotional habits are being converted into relatively permanent personality traits and into relatively permanent attitudes and beliefs.</u>

II. Recognition of Some Rules for Testing Right Thinking.

A. It is based on Objective Reality.

The objective is to remove from the picture that which comes from one's own imagination. By doing this, one's thoughts, feelings, and actions will be based on what is really happening. One will be guarded from unwarranted assumptions and jumping to conclusions.

B. <u>It Helps You to Achieve Your Goals</u>.

The Bible promises are given, among other reasons, to help our sinful unbelief which defeats us daily. As we think God's thoughts from His Word we are greatly benefited in our actions and attitudes.

C. It Keeps Us out of Conflict with others.

God's Word says, *as much as lieth in you, live peaceably with all men.* (Romans 12:18). Does your thinking on a particular issue keep you out of trouble or plunge you into it?

When scriptural principles are not compromised by giving in to the wishes of others in order to avoid conflict with them, it should be seriously considered as the course of action to take. Right and kind thinking does make a difference in life's relationships.

D. It Eliminates Significant Emotional Conflict.

As long as we are alive and conscious, there will be times when a conflict of interests will be experienced in our minds. The believer, for example, knows that if he allows the Holy Spirit to control his life this will involve him in a conflict with his old fleshly nature (Galatians 5:16, 17).

E. It Will Be Based Upon Spiritual Realities.

A believer, and even an unbeliever, needs to take into consideration the following spiritual realities: A Holy God, Jesus Christ, the Holy Spirit, Heaven, hell, judgment to come, and the love and grace of God. Meditation upon these things should greatly influence the life. In the case of an unbeliever, it is important that the Counsellor prayerfully explains the Word of God to them in order that they arrive at the Truth.

F. It is based upon Scriptural Principles.

Any thought, emotion or action that is contrary to the Word of God is spiritually irrational. Whether or not we understand God's ways, we still will find it pays to obey God's Word (Isaiah 55: 8, 9). Almost the whole history of Israel bears witness that people are not rational (or doing the rational and correct thing) when they disregard the Word of God.

III. Recognition of Common Irrational, Unbiblical Ideas.

These irrational ideas which people entertain in their thought life have a great impact on their life. The following are some of the irrational thoughts that are prevalent in the lives of many counsellees

- "I have a need to be loved or approved by almost everyone for virtually everything that I do". (Luke 6:26; Ephesians 1:6.)
- "I must be thoroughly competent, adequate, and highly achieving in all respects or I will be very unhappy with myself". Some think that if their performances are not nearly perfect, they are failures. (Romans 12:3-6; I Corinthians 12:14-18.)
- "It is terrible, horrible and catastrophic when things are not going the way I would like them to go." (Romans 8:28.) It is easy to exaggerate the importance of things such as mistakes or the achievements of other people. For some, a single negative event is considered a never-ending pattern of defeat, and for others, a single negative detail spoils everything.
- Human happiness is externally caused and people have little or no ability to control their sorrows or to rid themselves of their negative feelings. (Philippians 3:1; 4:4, 13.)
- If something is or may be dangerous or fearsome, you should be terribly occupied with it and upset about it, because that is normal. (Philippians 4: 6, 7)

- It is easier to avoid facing many of life's difficulties and self-responsibilities than to undertake some rewarding forms of self-discipline. (Galatians 6:5; Philippians 4:13)
- The past is all-important and because something once strongly affected your life, it should definitely do so now. (Philippians 3:13)
- You feel it, therefore it must be true; (Kings 19:10)
- People and things should be different from the way they are. (Romans 3:10; 8:7; II Timothy 3:1-4)
- Positive experiences don't count when you already have a negative belief. (Exodus 16:3) You can't foretell the future, so why not worry.
- Maximum human happiness can be achieved by inertia and inaction, or by passively and uncommittedly enjoying yourself, (John 15:10, 11)
- You can read people's minds. This is the basis for jumping to conclusions, (I Kings 5:11)
- By mislabeling something or someone with language that is highly coloured and emotionally loaded, you can actually change your evaluation of reality to be what you label it. (I Samuel 15:13, 20.) Many do this.

The Counsellor must also consider:

1. Accurate thinking will free a counsellee from the bondage of internal deception and gross generalities. Deception originated from Satan himself, the father of lies. Whenever Satan can cloud an issue or alter the truth, he can gain a foothold in the mind, (II Corinthians 10:3-5.)

2. Many people carry around lies in their minds as facts. The counsellor must help the counsellee to recognize those lies and replace them with the truth of the Word of God.
3. Most of this internal lying centres in self and comes from having accepted and believed false assumptions about self and God.
4. The Bible is the counsellor's textbook of truth; he must know it well and use it well. All that is said in the counselling interview must be evaluated in terms of the "thus saith the Lord."

HOMEWORK–AN AID TO HELP THE COUNSELLEE

Homework is one of the most important aspects of counselling. It is the exercise of homework that really brings about change. When homework ceases, true counselling ceases.

I. HELPING THROUGH HOMEWORK.

A. The Counsellee Needs Help as Well as Hope.

1. Homework will help uncover some of the basic problems from the past and in the present.
2. Homework will help the counsellee handle the problems that motivated him to seek counselling.
3. All problems must be considered important, genuine, and worthy of consideration.

B. Homework May be Geared at Re-educating.

Counsellees sometimes experience a feeling of disorientation which impairs their ability to think properly. They live according to impulse rather than according to God's commandments. They need carefully prepared homework assignments that will speak to their situation.

C. Counsellees need New Insights into their Problems.

They need to see that there is a potential for change. Written homework speeds up the counselling process, opens their minds to positively deal with their problems, and helps them to see and receive the answers according to God's Word.

D. Homework Clarifies Expectations.

   1. The counsellee sees clearly what is expected of him.
   2. He may only remember small parts of the counselling time, but the homework will open him up to the truth, and into new truth.
   3. Written assignments force the counsellor to be more concrete and more specific, and the counsellee to receive far more help.

E. Homework Sets a Pattern for Change.

   1. Homework must be expected from the beginning.
   2. It should accompany every session, or almost every session.
   3. It should be designed to lead to Biblical action and change. The counsellee needs to see change taking place in his life.

II. BENEFITS OF HOMEWORK.

A. Counselling Takes Place More Quickly.

Written homework speeds up counselling. Real change takes place during the week rather than during the session, and the high point becomes the homework rather than the session.

B. The Counsellee is Freed From Dependence Upon the Counsellor.

Directive counselling that instructs the counsellee to work at home, independently of the counsellor, is excellent. Homework helps the client to break loose-to stand on his own feet-to rely upon God, and not upon the counsellor. The counsellor is the coach, and the counsellee must learn to do much more for himself.

C. Homework Helps to r Gauge Progress or See the Lack of It.

It gives both the counsellor and counsellee a better idea of what is taking place. Without homework there will probably be very little progress or even an idea of what is required to bring about change.

D. Homework Allows the Counsellor to Deal With Problems.

1. The counsellor must set the stage for change. He does this by setting the Scriptural goals. He must design and assign the work.
2. In a truly Biblical sense he is the expert who aims to prescribe the Biblical method for change.
3. He must monitor the progress. He is able to spot potential problems and better deal with them as they are developing.
4. The holistic assessment form could be used in discerning problems and in monitoring progress. The use of priority lists and scheduling helps to reveal problems.

E. Homework Helps Regulate and Discipline the Counsellor's Counselling.

  1. It helps the counsellor to stay on track. As his goal is to bring about change through sanctification, he can know the extent to which he is succeeding.
  2. Weekly homework assignments keep the problem and the goals before the counsellor. It forces him to talk about solutions as well as problems and to bring about change. Homework will help the counsellor to eliminate talking in circles.
  3. It will drive home truth in the life of the counsellor as well, for he must search the Scriptures for the homework to be given.
  4. Homework provides a starting point for the next session. Each session can more easily build upon the last.

III. WHEN THERE IS FAILURE IN DOING HOMEWORK.

A. Questions which the counsellor may ask him/herself

  1. Was I thorough in giving the assignment? Did they understand what was really desired from them?
  2. Was there a lack of motivation? Were the counsellees simply disinterested? What can I do to motivate?
  3. Did the counsellees not find the time? What are their priorities? Do they understand the tremendous importance of their homework?

B. Maybe The Following Needs to Take Place.

  1. Write out the assignment so they totally understand it.

2. Have the counsellee repeat the assignment back, aloud, and ask if there are questions.

C. When They Fail, Do the Following.

1. Give the same assignment again.
2. Where possible, instruct the counsellee to go into another room and work on the assignment for 30 minutes. This also helps the counselle learn the importance of completing the assigned home work.

D. Understand the Failure.

Distinguish between unwillingness and legitimate obstacles that hinder the counsellee, or merely personal failure due to some personality weakness that also requires attention.

1. Have you granted forgiveness? It must be given or there will not be any future progress.
2. Is there hope? If there is no genuine hope, there also will not be any real change. Is the counsellee saved? Dead men have no power to change for the glory of God.

Has the counsellee been overcome by fear and worry? This will zap the energy that would otherwise be used to tackle the problem. The counsellor may have to disengage from going further until these problems are dealt with.

E. Counsellees Are Apt To Fail.

1. Learning new ways of living and building new habits can be challenging. Because of this the

client may be tempted to slide back. The counsellor must be there to help.
2. It will take firm, loving, straightforward sharing to bring change. There must be a lot of love but also honest sharing.
3. He must help the counsellee to call sin—sin. He should not minimize the problem. If the counsellor minimizes the problem the counsellee will minimize it also and will wonder if the counsellor really wants to help.

F. Failures can be turned into Opportunities.

1. He must see where he failed, why, and how to correct it. (The why(s) could include slothfulness, physical sickness, pride, loss of sleep, etc)
2. The counsellee can see his basic problems in a new light and possibly recoup by confession and reconciliation concerning this area of failure.

IV. SOME SAMPLES OF POSSIBLE HOMEWORK ASSIGNMENTS.

A. Write out a list of your sins. (Use Ephesians 4 as a guideline.)

B. Seek reconciliation with that offended brother/sister.

C. Write out a praise list. (Psalms 142, 145) or a think list, (Philippians 4:8) or a thank list. (Ephesians 5:19, 20.)

D. **Use the holistic assessment form and make a note of your anger outbursts.**

E. **And make up a schedule for your life**, and also a list of priorities. List those priorities in order of importance to you, and/or to God.

F. **Work on the homework assignments** using the Word of God as a reference book. These studies will get the counsellee into the Word of God for themselves.

G. **Write out questions you may have this week.**

H. **Attend Church and Sunday school regularly and begin a devotional life.** (Help the counsellee to begin a devotional notebook.)

I. **Memorize and outline certain portions of Scripture such as**, (Romans 13:14; II Corinthians 3:18; I Corinthians 6:11; 6:19-20)

CHAPTER SIX

COUNSELLING THE ADOLESCENT

The process of adolescence is sometimes considered complex, and it can be more challenging to define and understand what we should do for them as well as what their real needs might be.

It is during this time that young people experience many things that are unfamiliar to them, and they are growing up into independence and maturity, and sometimes growing away from their parents. They are making a move away from dependence into independence. This transition is sometimes perceived as a sign of rebellion and disrespect. However this is not always the case. Not all adolescents are in rebellion, or disturbed or at the mercy of their impulses, neither are they all resistant to parental values or rebellious. If they are understood and worked with properly, and the parent does not add to the problem by their own poor responses, they will experience positive changes. They are simply trying to adjust their lives to accommodate all the changes that are taking place in them.

As we think about this period of life it is good to remember that this transition is divided into three phases. There is early adolescence, middle adolescence and later adolescence. The Bible has a lot to say about adolescence, but, of course the word 'adolescent' does not appear in the Word of God and the term didn't come into use until about 1905 or 1910. Furthermore, adolescence was probably not recognized as a separate part of human development until about that time. At the turn of the century, it was recognized that adolescents were experiencing new freedoms which brought the need for a label that would designate the significance of that group and period of personal development.

The Bible does speak to young men and young women giving them many instructions for their lives.

<u>The period of early adolescence:</u> Early adolescence is the time that begins at about the age of ten or eleven and runs through the junior-high school years, (11-14). <u>It begins with a burst of biological changes</u> that often times cause anxiety, bewilderment and sometimes delight for the adolescent. This is the time the child often begins to feel awkward, self-conscious and many times very dissatisfied with their physical appearance. Their arms and legs grow long but their body seems to stay short, and pimples may appear on their faces. Such changes may come with challenges and bring bewilderment and concern. During this phase, they may also feel misunderstood.

This can also be the time when peer pressure and peer influence supersede that of their parents, teachers or others who they generally looked to as the source of inspiration and information. The input of peers becomes a significant factor in shaping their opinions and their lives.

<u>Insecurities may develop during this time</u>. They are transitioning from year 7 into junior-high, and so often they feel so insecure about making this move and the pressures which may arise with this transition. There is a kind of development akin to "chumship" that often develops during this period. It is great when this "chumship" is with one or both of the parents. But they generally become very intimate with their friends, and usually at this point, it is a same sex friend. Girls form very close friendships with other girls and boys form very close friendships with other boys. There is always the possibility of hero/celebrity worship and crushes on the opposite sex that comes into being during this period as well.

<u>There is a spirit of new independence</u> from parents which is very significant during this period of adolescence. This is and can be healthy but can also be misconstrued as rebellion by parents. Parents need to be educated not to see this attempt at independence as a rebellious spirit on the part of the child. Every adolescent is in the process of individualization, seeking to find their way. He is moving toward adulthood, and unless he is seriously challenging the value system of the family, this movement ought to be seen as normal and it

should not be viewed as a rebellious response on the part of the child.

The second phase is called middle adolescence. This is generally the period between the fifteenth and eighteenth year, while they are still in high school.

It is during this period of time that they are trying to adapt to their new identity as a person with an adult body, "growing away from childhood into adulthood" and dealing with the challenges and added responsibilities. During this period, sexual urges can be intense and difficult to control. In recent years there has been a staggering increase in the number of pregnancies among teenagers most of whom are unmarried.

<u>Peers begin to occupy a greater portion of their time</u> than ever. Sometimes, in particularly negative situations, the peer relationships can become overwhelming. Parents may be concerned that they are losing their child to peer relationships. It is natural for most youth that peer relationships become of greater significance during this time. This is why as a parent or as a counsellor it is extremely important that you help them to have the right kind of peers as their personal close friends. They need to be especially close to some peers who are going to help them maintain good values. They should be encouraged to attend a good church, and good youth groups are extremely important where young people really

love the Lord. The size of the group does not need to be large, but comprising of at least two or three other young people who will support the Biblical value system that is important to the child and their family.

Day dreaming is often a very common problem among young people and they may often spend a great deal of time in this activity. This can become a very serious thing if it takes up a significant amount of time especially when it is regarding desires, passions, etc., that may later cause sinful living. Sometimes day dreaming can be rooted in dissatisfaction with self or with their home, parents or siblings and it is a very unhealthy thing if it begins to take over the life of the youth. If not properly dealt with, this may continue in later life. The youth needs to deal with this problem and realize its seriousness, and must also be taught that f "what is being sown will be reaped." It is very important that the youth has healthy spiritual and mental attitudes, personal victory, and that they are kept busy enough to challenge the body, mind and soul.

Young men need to be very active physically to "siphon off" some of the urges that come from sexual desires that could be built by time spent in day dreaming. Lying in bed after awaking any length of time is not a healthy thing, or going to bed without sufficient physical weariness and thus allowing the devil and sin to take advantage is a very serious thing. The counsellor and parent must help the youth to understand and see the answers in the Word of God, which we will share later in this chapter to some extent.

It is <u>not uncommon for the youth</u>, at this period of life, to spend long hours on the phone. This is that period of adolescence when some spend long hours in their room, talking on the telephone with friends. <u>That kind of activity ought to be monitored by the parents</u>. If you don't let it get started or out of hand, you will not have as great a problem with it. Young people should not be allowed to make a "cave" out of their rooms. Nor should they be allowed to spend a great deal of time on the telephone.

Then <u>current teenage styles and fads are going to be strongly desired</u> during this period of their lives. It is a normal thing for the youth to want to conform, to be acceptable to those of his or her peer group. Strong parental loving concern and direction needs to be given during this period of time. Parents should take great care that they are not reactionary and drive the youth from them over little things that are just passing fads, and have little effect on the overall convictions of the home or the youth. Standards need to be maintained, for example, as to the kind of clothes and fads that are acceptable. But parents ought not to fear every fad. If a child ties a band around the head when they go out to jog does not mean that they are becoming a rebel. They should not react and fear every fad that is encountered.

Dating <u>and other relationships with the opposite sex become crucial</u> during the middle adolescence period. It is extremely important that parents work through their values and standards, including that of dating. Therefore make firm decisions first as parents. These things ought to be thoroughly taught to bring convictions prior to the time of dating so that the youth will be spared from actions and consequences which may result in heartache and potential ruin. Those who are teaching, or are parents, and give counsel to youth must have firm convictions of their own if they are going to help the youth. If you let a young couple go out on a date and there is no standard and no value that is placed on what time they are going to come home they will come home very late. You will be very unhappy and they will be very miserable about the confrontation that will probably take place. So make sure that standards are in place and they have convictions so by the time they reach this period of life they know what is going to be allowed and what is not going to be allowed.

<u>**Three** influences become extremely important</u> during the middle adolescent period.

1. <u>Sexual influence</u>. Biologically the middle adolescent is at the peak of his sexual energy. There is a need of love and acceptance in their lives. With the sexual openness that exists in our society today

there is an urgent need for a careful dialogue and careful teaching by the parent and those who counsel young people. There should be Biblical help so that youth avoid the pitfalls that our society has made and created with the sexual emphasis of this age.

2. <u>Problematic drugs use</u>. The counsellor, youth workers and parents will need to be extremely careful as they teach and direct in this area since drugs are so extremely prevalent in our culture. Parents should be cautioned to ensure that the youth are not involved with those who are in the drug scene. Convictions must be built in their life early on so they are spared of this scourge and the resulting ruin arising from "doing drugs".

3. <u>Driving and access to motor vehicles</u>. Sometimes, to the youth the car or a motorcycle provides a way to express power and give a boast to feelings of inferiority. As a result, they may express a desire to own a car, or a motorcycle. Careful decisions should be made about this. All these aspects need to be shared in counselling with the youth as they mature and their desires and wants grow.

Middle adolescents are faced with going to college, finding a job, leaving home and taking responsibility for their lives and future. It is often difficult for parents to loosen the "apron strings", so parents need to be encouraged and sometimes counselled about these matters. The youth require help and direction as they make God honouring decisions, and seek His will. (Ephesians 5:17; 5:10; 6:6; Colossians 4:12) Help them set Biblical standards for their lives.

Lastly, <u>it is natural for this age group to be asking the three basic questions</u>: "Why am I here?" "What can I do?" "Who am I?" They may be concerned about abilities, gifts, talents, and what to do about the future, or undergoing feelings of inferiority, loneliness, and a belief that no one understands them, while trying to get a grip on the purpose of life. Often in the midst of these things they are also testing and trying their parents as they endeavour to find out if the things the parents have stood for and taught are really true. Truth must become theirs in reality. Parents often misunderstand their teenager and think that the teenager is just being difficult when in actuality they are trying to find their way, and set their own convictions, purposes, and values in life. They must be encouraged to think for themselves, see the truth of God's Word, so that they do not fall into error. The counsellor must help the parents and those who work with the youth to understand some of these basic aspects of youth/adolescent development.

The last stage is called late adolescence. This is the period between graduation from high school and age 25—between the ages of 18-25)

<u>This is when the transition is made into adult society</u> and they begin to assume adult responsibility,

although they may still be living at home. Open, loving communication, respect, honour, and shared standards should be encouraged. It is important that they be counselled (the parents as well) that as long as they are in the home they keep the values and standards that are laid down as part of the functioning of the family unit. At the same time they may need counselling and encouragement to be working toward an independent status.

During this time <u>they may be formulating their own personal life style</u>. Parents should be encouraged to allow them the freedom to do that, however, the emerging styles and values should not be in conflict with the values and standards of the home, especially if there are small children in that home. The older youth must realize the importance of their own example and influence on the younger siblings. They must be led to a commitment in developing a life style that is congruent with the life style of that particular household and that is honouring to the Lord.

<u>There will be personal plans for the future</u>. Some may be thinking about marriage, and/ or moving into a career. They require nouthetic counselling and loving direction which can be extremely helpful during this period of time. But care should be taken by the parent or guardian (or counsellor) that a situation does not arise where it is perceived that they are being judged or their choices are being devaluated.

Such advice and direction can be extremely helpful, but it must be discreetly given to prevent a hostile relationship. Sympathetic understanding and heart felt listening should be encouraged.

The youth may also be <u>wrestling at times with feelings of inner emptiness, confusion, and inner personal tensions and anxiety</u>. Those who work with youth must be very careful to show that they care, they love them, and to give them the input they need about how to make the most out of their lives. They must remember that this group is trying to "nail down" some questions that are basic to their lives. They are considering...

1. Who am I?
2. How do I relate to others?
3. What should I believe? and
4. What should I do with my life?

They are really wrestling with these four areas and need help and direction toward answers in the Word of God without appearing in any way to invade their privacy. Allow them the space to come to the knowledge of the truth in God's Word and avoid being "pushy".

SOME BIBLICAL CONSIDERATIONS AND APPLICATIONS TOWARDS THE NEEDS OF ADOLESCENTS

The Bible has a lot to say that is applicable to all stages of the youth's development. The Word of God does speak to young men and women giving them very definite direction and instruction for their lives.

They are urged to be overcomers. In the book of I John 2:14 (2:12-14) we read of three groups of people, designated as "men, children and young men". Probably the term "young men" does not necessarily mean men who are a certain age in their youth. It probably does mean those who are of various ages, but who are like young men in that they show three characteristics in their spiritual development. But let's apply it to youth! It instructs young men and women to incorporate the Word of God into their beings. They are to be strong in the Word, for it must become the engrafted word, and dwell in their spirit and hence in their lives; (Colossians 3:16; James 1:21) Also they are told that they are to overcome Satan, whenever temptation arises. The young person must learn to resist the devil and overcome his wiles, darts, and onslaughts; (James 4:7; I John 2: 12-17; I Peter 5:8, 9; Ephesians 6:10-18)

Youth are counselled to "flee" from certain things.

The Word of God clearly urges the youth to flee certain things as the basic answer when temptation comes and the urges to sin are there. They are to

1. Flee youthful lusts, (II Timothy 2:22);
2. Flee fornication, (I Corinthians 6:18), for the Greek word means all kinds of sexual sins;

3. Flee idolatry or the allowing of idols of any kind including covetousness, (I Corinthians 10:14; Luke 12:15);

   4. Flee these things, (I Timothy 6: 9, 10) and "following after righteousness, godliness, faith, love, patience, meekness." (I Timothy 6:11, 12)

   5. Flee strangers, (John 10:5) or false and wrong kind of leaders.

If our youth, during the various stages of their development apply the Scriptures and truly seek to "flee" as God commands, much of the failure and fall into sin would be alleviated. God means exactly what HE says, and that is "to flee" as the answer to temptations.

We are to literally run from and stay away from areas of potential temptations and failure. Those who work with youth must help them to make this a habit of their lives.

<u>Young people are urged to be submissive to their elders</u>. (I Peter 5:5) In Titus 2:4 the late adolescent is admonished to love their spouses and to be taught by the older generation to fulfil God's will and desires for their lives. The young men are to be taught to be "serious minded, in all things shewing thyself a pattern of good works; in doctrine shewing uncorruptness, gravity, sincerity, sound speech, that cannot be condemned..." (Titus 2:6-8) The aged women are to teach the young women certain things ..."to be sober, to love their husbands, to love their children, to be discreet, chaste, keepers at home, good, obedient to their own husbands, that the word of God be not blasphemed." (Titus 2: 4, 5) In II Peter 5:5-7 they are exhorted to humble themselves under the Mighty Hand of God.

In probably one of the most quoted portions to youth, **they are urged to be an example to the believers**. (I Timothy 4:12) Here they are urged to so conduct themselves as to not have a reproach upon their person, and therefore be despised. Those who work with the youth must do their best to help young people build a Godly life and be an example of saving faith in their daily lives. These characteristics are greatly needed in our youth today.

There are many things that the word of God has to say to adolescent and they are designed to speak to them where they are apt to have particular problems. The counsellor, youth worker and parent must be very familiar with the Scriptures, make a thorough study of the word of God looking for applications to daily living, and have firm convictions so that they can indeed help the young people of today in this difficult age.

AREAS WHERE ADOLESCENTS FACE THEIR GREATEST PROBLEMS

What are the areas in which the youth are experiencing great challenges as they move through the transitional stages into their early twenties? What are the causes of the problems for those adolescent years?

There are the difficult physical changes. During most of those years the youth face many physical changes. I think every adult ought to be sympathetic toward the adolescent and understand the tremendous physical as well as physical changes they are going through. This growth spurt is often accompanied by skin problem, fat, and periodical increases in energy and changes in body proportions. There is the development of body hair, changes of the voice, and other physical changes that can be tremendously embarrassing and frustrating to the youth. Jokes from adults about the changes taking place in the adolescent's life are most inappropriate. Late bloomers or those late in maturing are often the objects of jokes as are early bloomers, and care needs to be taken about the changes, and sensitivity needs to be shown as well. Love and support from adults who are around them is very important.

Hormonal changes are also taking place at a very rapid pace. The emotional changes that accompany the hormonal changes can bring about feelings of fear, confusion, anger, hostility, or great temptation. There may be guilt and depression over sinful thoughts and acts. Sensitivity as well as encouragement is required by the adults around them. We need to be extremely encouraging. Those who work and support the youth must help embrace the Biblical admonitions to Holy living. (II Timothy 2:22; I Thessalonians 4:3-7; I Corinthians 5:9-11; 6:8-20)

<u>Many young people go through a period when</u> **they struggle with morals, ethics and religion**. They may question whether they really hold to and accept the values of their parents and their churches. This should be seen as a normal part of their developmental cycle. Parents should answer such questions sincerely and honestly, in accordance with the Word of God. In the day when television has such a great impact on lives, there are a lot of false concepts about what is right if they have been greatly influenced by the media. Secular music has also influenced a lot of the youth, those who work with youth as well as adults, should have a strong sense of the standards set for God honouring music. Those who work with young people need to help them toward convictions early in life that will "anchor them" when they are confronted by the temptation to seek or accept the wrong ideals of their secular peers. (I Timothy 4:12; Prov. 2:1-11; Proverbs 6:22-23)

<u>Inner personal relationships</u> are often a problem to young people in all three stages of adolescent development. Both boys and girls can be great friends one day and then struggle with one another the next day. They need to see consistency in their lives and in the lives of those around them as well as the stabilizing factor which comes through good communication, those living out God's Word, whether or not in authority. All those who work with the youth must help them to understand the need to build friendships with the right kind of persons.

Independence is a real issue during this period. Many parents have a hard time "letting go" of their young person. Mothers may especially try to keep them "tied to their apron strings". Rather than enjoying the experience of seeing their young person maturing and enjoying communication with them now on a more adult level, parents sometimes struggle with the transition their children are undergoing.

Sometimes adolescents appear to demand too much independence too quickly. This matter of independence is something that must be negotiated and parents need to listen to their youth and convince the youth of the importance of listening to the parents as well. The parent must realize that the child may appear to grow away from them but in reality are seeking to understand life and their new responsibilities and experiences as they grow older, but draw back toward them in respect, loyalty and sharing of life as they develop and get into the mid- twenties, if not at least in their early thirties. This is a period of time that they are trying to find themselves and all that goes with their new-found adulthood.

Many teenagers (and those in early twenties) sometimes struggle with self-identity or with self-esteem and self-image. This can cause a lot of problems during the adolescent years as they wrestle with who they are, and how they feel about themselves. If they experience a poor self-image in their childhood they may experience some problems during these years and their adult life, if not dealt with properly. For the saved person, our self-image and self-identity should be "wrapped up" in who we are and what we have in Christ Jesus. Our acceptance is in Christ, and in Him and because of Him we can rejoice in the truth of unconditional love (Ephesians 1:6; John 15:9; Colossians 3:1-4; II Corinthians 1:30)

The future is a source of great concern to many young people today. They may be concerned and fantasise about the future. What is going to happen in the future? What will happen to them in the coming years? Current events and the many negative things taking place in the world and around them may cause concern. They may also be concerned about their financial future as adults and parents. Again, great encouragement and the positive input of the Word of God are needed in their lives. They need to study good books that will give them a basis of considering the future and financial matters.

CHAPTER SEVEN

YOUTH'S RESPONSES TO THEIR PROBLEMS

There are many ways that these problems affect adolescences. They will also hold a variety of responses to these problems as well.

Some will begin to hold in their problem. They will cease dialoguing and communicating with those around them. This engenders loneliness and a lot of day dreaming, feeling of worthlessness, and a feeling of alienation and withdrawal from friends and parents. There can be apathy, a forsaking of usual interests and activity, or a perpetuating of inner turmoil. This is unhealthy and can be a source of grief and anxiety to the parents.

For some it is the opposite as they "act out" their problems. The use of alcohol, drug abuse, lying, stealing, violence, crime and gang behaviour is related to the fact that the adolescent is experiencing a tremendous amount of turmoil and he or she is acting out their frustrations. Often times, if the inner needs are met and the youth have a good self-image and good relationships with the authority figures in their lives, this situation will never arise. Too often parents are too busy and neglect their youth, do not keep the lines of communication open and the young person is acting out their sinful ways to try and hurt the parent for the many things that have caused them pain. They perceive that they are not loved and the parent does not really care for them or what happens to them.

It is often noted that adults also "act out" their problems rather than deal with the sin and the, and determine by God's grace to have the victory that is available in Christ. In a later section we give some suggestions about this matter.

It is common for society **to try to escape from the problem, finding alternative means to "control" it rather than deal with the matter head on**. Husbands and wives separate and divorce, rather than deal with the situation. Youth run away and when they do so they run away from the protection of their family and society. Often, they fall into the hands of predators, very evil and malicious people who are looking for the young "run-away" and then their problem intensifies. This not only occurs within the secular society, but also in the Christian society as well.

Alternatively, there are those who stick with their problems. They will discuss them with their friends or trusted adults, trying harder to learn from their mistakes and move through the period of adolescence in a relatively smooth fashion, provided they have the Biblical help and much encouragement to cope with their problems, and have the "role models" that will strengthen such actions. They need Biblical answers, and they must have convictions in their lives prior to the times of great stress, so they can stand when the pressures are there.

SUGGESTIONS FOR THE COUNSELLOR AND OTHERS WHO WORK WITH ADOLESCENTS

Between the parents and the youth there can be feelings of confusion, disappointment, hurt, anger, anxiety and even much guilt.

<u>The counsellor needs to **be extremely sensitive, calm, compassionate and mature enough to tolerate criticism or flattery**</u>. In counselling the parents, the counsellor needs to encourage them with support and with facts that most teenagers do go through these things and most of them do need to be given some freedom to think independently. Parents also need to understand that the youth need goals put before them and the parents must set the goals. They must also understand that while each member of the home has rights yet there must be a setting of limits in order that the youth will not go beyond certain limits. The youth needs to be taught to respect the rights and interests of all concerned. The parents need to respect the rights and interests of the young person as well and help them manifest real spiritual maturity as a role model for those young people. Most often spiritual maturity will be more "caught" than "taught" during those adolescent years. If you as a parent are giving all kinds of evidence that you cannot trust

God, or that you cannot trust them you will probably do more to injure their spiritual development than anything else that could happen to them.

Often the adolescent will have questions. But those questions will be heightened if parents meet those questions with a real spirit of criticalness or over legalistic or in a judgmental position. The counsellor must encourage the parents to manifest a high degree of spiritual maturity and to be careful in how they work with the youths.

When counselling **the adolescent the counsellor must first get into the business of building rapport**. Time must be spent to build rapport and a good relationship with the youth. The counsellor must create a receptive atmosphere so the adolescent knows you are willing to listen to him, that you are going to be sensitive and open to what he (she) has to say. Honesty and respect mixed with gentle firmness must be given. The counsellor must deal directly with resistance and confront the young person about it. Inform him that he is developing a resistant attitude and allow him to express himself but keep things positive. Focus on discussion and concrete issues. Periodically take the time to summarize or point out what is happening emotionally within the session and always listen to the adolescent and give him (or her) the right and the responsibility for giving you feedback about what is going on.

The counsellor must **be sensitive to the issue of transference** as it applies to the counselling relationship. This refers to the tendency of individuals to transfer feelings about another person they have met in their life in the past to the person in the present, or more specifically to the counsellor during the counselling session. The young person may be transferring their hostility and feelings about their father or mother to you. Again be sensitive to this as it will have to be dealt with. Let the youth know you are not his father and you are not his grandfather, or some other adult toward whom he may have hostilities. You are a concerned adult who is trying to listen and trying to help. Be careful you don't respond like the person with whom you are being compared. When you think you have identified who that person is, make certain you are not reacting as you sense they may have reacted.

As stated previously, **you will need to get into "problem identification"**. You will need to encourage the youth to talk about life issues they are currently dealing with such as: school, leisure activities, their home, their parents, their religious life and experiences, their plans for the future, their dating, their sexual problems if there are any, their likes and their dislikes, their worries, their relationships with siblings, etc. You must try to get into all of these aspects as you dialogue with the adolescent but also being a friend instead of an interrogator. Don't get so heavy into questions that you look like an investigator, or private detective. Show your desire to listen and be alert while listening to what the person has to share.

Set goals, stimulate self-understanding and build communication; do all these in order to select the goals to focus on during the counselling sessions. You will need to introduce the concept of some "contracting"; entering into contractual agreement with the adolescent i.e. getting them to commit to achieving the set goals in order to produce the desired results. You will need to have some specific goals in mind; actions that will improve:

1. his relationship with his parents
2. his relationship with his teachers
3. his ability to function within his peer group
4. self-image.
5. how he deals with the issues that have caused guilt.

There are a number of Biblical truths that need to be considered. The youth needs to understand if he or she is really a Christian. Does he really understand Biblical grace, Biblical forgiveness? Does God seem to him (in his mind) to be sort of a cosmic policeman? If the person is not saved, then seek to lead them to Christ. We need to clarify God with the young person in order to be certain they are not holding unto false concepts about the person of God. Clarify grace and sin, clarify the "sowing and reaping" process (Galatians 6:7-9), putting much emphasis on this if you know they are truly saved, and help them understand the importance of considering what they are sowing, and what their harvest is and will be. Clarify the importance of personal choices, clarify forgiveness and make sure that by the time they leave the counselling relationship they thoroughly understand all these Biblical concepts and how to deal with temptation and walk in personal.

Then we need to consider some ways to make the counselling as effective as possible. Any one of these or a number of these methods (and others as well) may work to help counsel the youth with whom you are working.

1. There are times when "one on one" counselling with the youth is the most effective.
2. There are other times when you will need to meet with the parents along with the adolescent. Sometimes, parents must be there to help clarify and/ or be counselled in areas where they are involved.
3. At times nothing could be more effective than a group of adolescents sitting around, discussing and dealing with one another, in what they call "rapping", with the adult counsellor keeping things moving in the right direction. You want to lead them as a group to help them consider the important topics and the goals of the peer discussion as well as help them find Biblical conclusions to various aspects of their problems.

PREVENTING PROBLEMS OF THE ADOLESCENT YEARS

Build a strong foundation in their childhood. There are things that we can do to help prevent problems in the first place. One of the most important aspects is what I call "Preventive Discipline". We need to labour to build conviction in the first place so that the youth has such strong convictions that they are spared from sin when certain temptations come into their lives as a result of the maturing years. This is done by encouraging, admonishing, training, teaching, , exhorting, etc., unto the end to bring strong convictions based on the word of God. (Proverbs 2:1-11; 3:1-8; 4:1-3; 4:10-13; 4:20-23; 6:20-23; 7:1-3)

The best way to prepare the youth is to build their lives when they are still children. During childhood, be consistent, be firm, and loving, have some rules but don't be legalistic, be democratic, be a negotiator, be open, but still ensure a proper spiritual foundation for the child. Don't allow the child to manipulate or control you, and yet be loving and careful in the way that you handle the child. Keep active, vital family devotional lives helping the child to see how the word of God applies to their lives, keep active in Church, and have a constant and consistent input on a spiritual level.

Educate them about certain specifics. You need to talk to or counsel young people about such issues as sexuality, drinking, masturbation, pregnancy, drug abuse, etc., All these things and more need to be discussed normally within the family unit. If parents are embarrassed about these things there are problems that are going to develop later. We need to educate our children about these things and then also send them to a Christian school. It is not a panacea, there are problems there, but there are teachers who are going to consistently uphold the values that are being taught in the home. Parents must teach many aspects of daily living and again build convictions in the lives of the children and teenagers so that they will determine to live for Christ.

Parents must keep a good family example. Counsellors must help the parents to see the importance of giving the greatest gift; a stable home environment for that child and adolescent. Often that will do more to help the adolescent to turn out right than anything else. The youth needs to see a modelling of communication and of commitment more than anything else. That will be tremendously helpful. There needs to be consistent, Godly living with Biblical principles being applied and lived in the nitty-gritty of daily life.

They need a lot of inner-personal support. The church and the Christian school can stimulate good friendship. Give direction, give spiritual teaching, help them to establish the right kind of friends and have the right kind of fun. Parents can help their youth to get involved with a peer group that they approve of, preferably one within a church or Christian ministry that they are also associated with. Choose your children's friends, you can't always do it blatantly or forcefully, but you can do a lot of that "under the table" so to speak, as you help them to develop the right kind of friends. More than any other reason youth go astray because of the wrong kind of close friends. If their peer group are unsaved, sold out to sin and the world, you can be sure your child will be greatly influenced by such a group.

If we do all these things and teach parents along these lines, and counsel in this manner, one will have a reasonably effective counselling ministry with adolescents though it won't be all smooth sailing. Besides, there is no such thing as a smooth sailing counselling ministry with adolescents. But it will be effective, you will be fulfilled doing it, and at the end, you will realize that when the youth move into their adult lives they will be well adjusted having a background of helpful counsel that will put them in good stead.

CHAPTER EIGHT

COUNSELLING ANGRY, UNMOTIVATED, SELF-CENTERED, AND SPIRITUALLY-INDIFFERENT TEENAGERS

(This chapter is an extract of Dr Tony Ogefere's diary, with permission)

Counselling angry and indifferent young people typically begins with presenting issues. But counselling does not stop there. The <u>youth counsellor</u> who tries to identify the teenager's problem for him and then offers his own solutions, even his understanding of Biblical solutions, does not have to wait very long— maybe five or ten minutes—to see the counselling session fail. The teenager tunes out the counsellor with polite tolerance, impatient for the session to end. Most often he does not return for a second interview. The angry teenager believes that most adults who try to help do two things. They pick the problem(s) to work on, and then offer solutions they believe will resolve the problem. In such a session, the teenager mentally checks out in short order.

One mother brought her teenager to me for counselling and complained, "John is just so unmotivated. He won't do anything that is good for him. He's grounded. He can't use the car. He's on academic probation. He is ineligible for wrestling. And he can't go out with his girlfriend. Nothing motivates him. We've even severely limited how much he can be at his job, which he loves. Nothing seems to work."

I looked at John and asked if his parents had imposed all of these consequences on him. He responded with a matter-of-fact "Yes."

I sat back, looked at his mum and asked, "Could I share with you another way to look at John?"

She said, "Go ahead."

I continued. "John, I don't mean to show disrespect to your mother, but I couldn't disagree with her more. I've never seen a student more motivated than you!"

He leaned forward a bit. I had captured his interest. His mother was genuinely perplexed.

"You're grounded and can't go out with friends, right?"

He nodded agreement.

"You lost time at your job because of your grades, right? You can't use the car. You're on academic probation making you ineligible for wrestling. And you can't go out with your girlfriend."

"Yeah, that's right."

I looked at him and at his mother, paused, and then asked, "So with all this restriction you still do the things that made you lose these privileges. Is that what I hear your mum say, John?"

He thought about his response and then slowly nodded agreement with my description of the situation.

"That is remarkable motivation," I said. "You want something so badly that you have committed yourself to enduring remarkable pain and loss in order to get it. That is serious dedication, not lack of motivation. I can only imagine what could be done in your life, John, if you decided to use that kind of intensity and commitment to get things that could benefit you instead of things that bring loss and trouble."

John was motivated—but not to do what his mother, the youth pastor, teachers, or I wanted, regardless of how noble, beneficial, or painful these goals seem. He was not even motivated to do what God wanted. He was motivated to pursue his own "wants." Just because a young person is not motivated to go after the things the adults in his life want him to pursue, one cannot conclude that he is not motivated. All teenagers, no matter how indifferent to parental or school goals, are highly motivated.

Start with the Teenager's "Wise Wants"

If I am going to help John, I must tune into what he wants on two levels: first, what he is aware that he wants, and second his "wise wants"—his motives that contain some wisdom. If I can detect these "wise wants," I may be able to help John see how he can get what he "wisely wants" by making Biblically-principled choices. At the same time, I may be able to show John how his current actions now torpedo the very things he does want.

Solomon, in his proverbial counsel, presumes that motives are a part of us, even though we may not be aware of them. "A man's ways seem right to him but motives are judged by the LORD" (Proverbs 18:3). We all act. We all have thoughts about our acts. And we all have motives for our acts and thoughts. This verse does not give carte blanche approval to all motives. In fact, all our motives are contaminated by sin. But at this deeper level, because of God's creation and common grace, other biblical testimony assumes that some of our motives contain some measure of wisdom.

We can fruitfully counsel young people who are committed to their wants by detecting and affirming their underlying "wise wants." These are the desires, motives, longings and wants that God has created as part of our human nature. For sure, it is ultimately God's purposes that the teenager needs to pursue. It is God's truth that will set the teenager free. It is also the teenager's common self-centredness that distorts his perspective about his problems and the real solutions to them. The purpose of this chapter is to show that the way to get a teenager to these points of conviction is to begin, as Scripture does in its model of youth ministry, in Proverbs with his "wise wants."

"Wise Wants"—a Scriptural Precedent for Beginning Youth Counselling

God's approach to young people, as pictured in the wisdom literature, shows that the young person's interests are wise starting places for the counsellor. In Proverbs, wise counsel to angry, foolish, or indifferent young people begins with apparent solutions to the desires and goals they already have. The vast majority of the proverbs make certain assumptions about the motivations of young adults. "Lazy hands make a man poor, but diligent hands bring wealth" (Proverbs 10:4) assumes that teenagers want to avoid poverty and acquire wealth. "A man is praised according to his wisdom, but men with warped minds are despised" (Proverbs 12:8) assumes that young people want praise, approval, and respect and do not want the opposite. These desires are "wise wants."

"Wise wants" inform the counsel in Proverbs. Presumably youth desire to have a reputation for trustworthiness and honour; parents who are proud of them and joyful because of them; healthy friendships, including delightful romance; a sense of security and confidence; usefulness in the lives of others; and competence and success in work. Other proverbs assume that young people want to be discerning and thoughtful; to use good judgment; to be able to respond effectively to others' questions and demands; to combat laziness, selfishness, anger, lying, and lust; and to not be seduced, exploited, deceived or misled. God has programmed these desires, or "wise wants" into teenagers—into all of us. Counsel to young people can build upon these wants the same way Proverbs' crisp counsel does. But youth counsellors must first of all identify the teenager's "wise wants," then see how these wise wants have been distorted by the folly of youthfulness.

Parents and other authorities often react to the teenager's foolish choices and miss his "wise wants." This confusion is furthered by the faulty assumption that what the teenager wants—as reflected in his immediate choices, words, or patterns of behaviour—is what he really wants. But most teenagers do not see where their choices lead. They do not live with an "eschatological perspective"—the big picture of how their decisions impact their future and God's purposes for them. They are here-and-now people, just as Proverbs assumes them to be. What did John want so badly that it made him willing to dig in his heels, and at great personal cost, refuse to do anything his parents and teachers wanted him to do? The counsellor has to ask this question. The counsellor has to be geared to listen for the "wise want," now distorted into foolish desires that direct the young person's choices.

"What do you want?" Is a powerful and critical question in youth counselling. Answers vary but give clues to wise wants. "I just want to graduate and get out of here." "I want my parents to get off my back." "I just want to talk to children about the Lord—all this academic stuff means nothing." "I just want to do what I want to do when I want to do it." Are there any wise wants behind these statements? Or is the counsellor duty-bound to confront the teenager with his rebellion, self-centredness, disrespect, and laziness? All of these may be features of John's heart right now. But there is more to John than just these sinful responses.

Start by talking to this teenager about how his stubbornness and disrespect can wreck his life and see how long you have his attention. Do this even with politeness and gentleness. The young person will not take long to realize whose wants are being addressed—and that they certainly are not his wants. There is more to look at than just the sin in counselling youth— as important as that is. The issue is not, "Do we deal with the sin or do we not?" The issue is when and how do we deal with the sin.

Let's go back to my conversation with John. If I keep his "wise wants" in mind, I might say something like this:

> John, I want to commend you for having such a high level of commitment to your own

goals. I respect that so much. You are not willing to be moved from the place you've settled into for anything or anybody. That level of determination is rare in many young adults. Furthermore, I think I sense a real spirit of independence in you. That, too, is a mature goal. Are these the things I'm hearing you say you want?

I guess so.

How else would you describe what you want out of your relationship with your parents and your time here at school?

I just want to be able to make my own decisions.

That is a very mature desire, John. You want the freedom to make your own choices and to accept responsibility for your own life. Is that what you are saying?

Yes, I'm old enough to make my own decisions. But they keep treating me like a child.

Do you know where these desires for maturity, commitment, independence, and the sense of responsibility come from?

What do you mean?

Well, John, these desires have been created within you. They are not wrong in themselves. God has built these interests in you as one created in His image. I respect your desire to make your own decisions, to be independent, and to be committed to the way of living that you've set as a goal for yourself. But, let me ask you a question. Is the way you are handling things at school and at home getting you the independence and freedom that you want?

Well, no, not right now.

In this brief conversation, I have touched on John's wise wants. I listened carefully to John so that I could convey the fact that he's not being talked into something that he does not want. John lets me lead him because I focus on his wants. John is motivated to do what will get him what he wants and to avoid what will block his goals.

"Wise Wants" and Self-centredness

Is it possible that this appeal could encourage or reinforce John's self-centredness? Could this approach set up John to manipulate his parents or others to get what he wants? The answer is yes on both counts. But in spite of these possibilities, the sages of Proverbs forge ahead with their pointed solutions-oriented counsel. They advise young people how to acquire what they wisely want—and what they certainly need. It is true that the counsellors of Proverbs do this in the bigger context of the "fear of the Lord" (Proverbs 1:7; 9:10). But while "the fear of the Lord" is the heart orientation that ought to control all choices, it seems to be a stretch to say that a teenager's commitment to the fear of the Lord is the necessary condition in Proverbs for giving him wise counsel. The statement "A gentle answer turns away wrath, but a harsh word stirs up anger" is good advice for both a Godly person and an ungodly person. Similarly, "…humility comes before honour" can bring God's favour to a pagan like King Nebuchadnezzar or to a Godly young man like Samuel who fears the Lord.

The counsel in Proverbs is not only for parents to discuss with teenagers whose hearts are right with the Lord. Our deep desire is for all our teenagers' changes to emerge from hearts that love Christ. We know that Godly counsel must ultimately address the teenager's heart. But the journey that nurtures an angry teenager's Godly choices usually does not begin by early steps in which we talk about his need to love and follow Christ. In time, our ministry setting may let us go there, but often it cannot start there.

Throughout Scripture, God imparted good sense, logical thinking, and wise decision-making abilities to kings and others who were not interested in the fear of the Lord. His counsel usually centred on their self-preservation, prosperity, health, and welfare. God gave wisdom to Nebuchadnezzar of Babylon, Cyrus of Persia, Pharaoh and the tutors He provided for Moses, the Roman officials in Jesus' time, Saul's teacher Gamaliel, and people without number throughout Biblical history. In addition, God allowed them to prosper as a result—even though many of them used His benefits for their own personal kingdom building:

to enhance their pride, fuel their arrogance, and exploit God's people. In the process, they stored up judgment for themselves (Roman 2:5) while they abused God's kindness to them. But their misuse of God's goodness did not restrain His generous provisions to them. Even Jesus took note of this when He taught about love for neighbours—and enemies, saying, "He [God] causes His sun to rise on the evil and the good...So love your enemies..." (Matthew 5:43ff).

Biblical youth counsellors need to recognize that they are in a position to love the rebellious, indifferent, angry adolescents in front of them. One way to do this is to begin with the teenager's "wise wants" and show him how to satisfy these wants. Conversely, we can also love them by showing them how their poor choices can lead to more of the loss, pain, or trouble they are experiencing—just the opposite of what they want—"ruin" or a life that is "hard" (Proverbs 13:15). God uses our good works (our helpful counsel), along with His own acts of kindness (John 6:35-38), to lead people to repentance and to show them His glory (Roman 2:4; Matthew 6:16).

Draw Attention to "Exceptions"

When a teenager realizes how he can get what he wants, he is often willing to put himself through a great deal of trouble to get it. Therefore, the strategies a counsellor uses to effect change in a young person will be most productive if these strategies grow out of the teenager's own experiences and goals. Counsellors can help a teenager identify wise things he's done in the past, by God's common grace, that have produced some of what he wisely wants. These "exceptions" are different, Biblically-wise things he has said or done in the past that have produced more favourable outcomes than the ones he is getting now. Often these past situations involve some of the same people or events in his present situation.

For example, in the past, Afua talked respectfully to her mum and enjoyed the privileges of going out with her friends. Now she's grounded. In the past James did his homework and was able to play basketball. Now he's ineligible. In the past Seth kept his room clean, came in on time, and helped his dad with work around the house. As a result he had a great relationship with his dad. Now they fight all the time. In the past Diana showed interest in other new students in school and made friends. Now she's lonely.

Drawing attention to exceptions like these can shift the counselling from being problem-centred to being solution-centred. By doing this, the counsellor sees the big picture of human nature, as Proverbs does. He talks to the teenager about solutions in light of the young person's identity as one created in the image of God with life experiences he can draw upon. These solutions typically yield rapid change and movement toward the teenager's goals because they are his own ideas about what has helped him get what he has wanted in the past. Most important, though, a solutions approach allows the counsellor to be positive and affirming to the teenager without being patronizing or manipulative. Godly youth counsellors can genuinely recognize commendable qualities in students—their wise wants and their wise exceptions. This commonly produces trust and a close relationship with the counsellor which sets the stage for the most important counselling yet to be done: movement beyond this focus on self toward matters of the heart (idolatry, repentance, submission to Christ, and a life of faith and worship).

Most counselling and confrontation with angry young people focus on the teenagers' negative behaviour. This "wise-wants," solution-oriented approach avoids the defensiveness, blame shifting, and turned-off feeling of teenagers suddenly confronted with their sin. It does not overlook or minimize sin, which must eventually be addressed. But getting to heart issues can start from the outside—with the concerns of the young person.

Is this the old Rogerian, self-sufficient, "I have the answers to all my problems within me" anthropology? No. The "wisdom of the organism" (Roger's term) will never be sufficient to stand the weight of the troubles of this life or of the life to come. Counsellors can acknowledge that the teenager, by

God's common grace, has made some wise choices in the past and can use these past experiences to point the teenager toward true freedom.

The uncommon nature of this approach to teenagers often catches them off guard. Their typical resistance and knee-jerk reaction to adult counsel—even nice, loving confrontation— disappears. Now they are forced to think about their choices and not about "the enemy." Teenagers realize that the counsellor is not the enemy talking to them, and you are commending them, not condemning them. You are not trying to change them. You are identifying the wise wants of students, who will sense that you are going to help them to be discerning about how to fulfill their wise desires. You do not minimize sin. You simply wait until the teenager appears to have ears to hear, when your ideas are more likely to be heard—after rapport and trust have been built between you and the young person. "The tongue of the wise commends knowledge…" (Proverbs 15:2) and "A wise man's heart guides his mouth, and his lips promote instruction" (Proverbs 16:23).

Temporal Consequences: The Sages' Cache of Weapons for Change

Wholeness will only come to a young person as his heart is transformed and as he seeks first the kingdom of God. But to get him to that deep spiritual place, the sages of Proverbs offer nearly 700 examples of positive and negative temporal consequences for wise or foolish decisions. The true "beginning" or principal part of wisdom is the "fear of the LORD" (Proverbs 9:10). But there are degrees of wise living that even dumb animals and insects such as ants, coneys, locusts, and lizards exhibit (Proverbs 30: 24-28). Similarly, young people, even unbelieving ones, can practice some degree of wise living that will come back to reward them (Proverbs 9:12) and may lead them to repentance (Romans 2:4).

Case Summary

In the following case summary, the counsellor listens for what the teenager does not want (the problem), clarifies what she wisely does want (wise wants—the goal), looks for exceptions (immediate, temporal solutions), helps her plan her choices (her "wise" strategy), then leads her thinking toward her own heart needs. The setting is my Church office, but could just as easily be a restaurant or ball game with a youth leader or parent.

> Warimu, a fresh student, had just transferred to a local school from another school in Birmingham. I had gotten to know Warimu a little when her mother teacher in her school referred her to me.
>
> Warimu stormed into my office.
>
> She's so unfair! She takes points off for my maths homework even when I get the right

answers. I don't understand why she's so picky. I do the problems the way I was taught in my last school and I get the right answer. But that's not good enough for Mrs. Smith. She wants things done her way only. That's not right!

You're pretty upset about this aren't you, Warimu?

Yeah. She is so unreasonable. My last maths teacher taught us to do it a different way and I understand it. It makes more sense than the way she wants us to do it. But she won't let me do it my way—even though I get the right answer."

You don't have to do it her way, Warimu.

I don't?"

No, you can do the problems your way. In fact you don't have to do the problems at all, if you don't want to.

I don't?

Warimu paused a few seconds. Then, as though she recognized that there would be a price to pay for doing it her own way, Warimu said,

Yeah, but she'll take points off and I want to get a good grade in maths.

Yes, she probably will take points off.

But that's not fair. She shouldn't be able to do that.

Maybe she shouldn't, but can you control that?

No, I can't.

So you have a choice. You can do the work the way Mrs. Smith wants it done and earn the points or you can refuse to do it Mrs. Smith's way and have points taken off.

But that's not fair!

Maybe not. But what do you want me to do?

Change Mrs. Smith.

Me? Change her? Who am I? Teachers are in charge of their own classroom procedures. I have no authority in her teaching. The principal won't make a teacher change his or her teaching methods as long as nothing is wrong with what she is doing.

Yeah, but my grade will go down.

That's probably true. So, Warimu, what do you want? It sounds like you've identified two ways things can go: you can get points by doing it her way and earn a stronger grade, or you can lose points and earn a weaker grade by doing it your way. What do you think you want to do? You can do whatever you want.

Warimu thought over her options. While she was mulling things over, I said,

Warimu, have you ever been in a situation where you've chosen to do something someone in authority wanted you to do, even though you wanted to do something different?

Yes, I think so.

Tell me about it.

Yeah. My dad wanted me to clean my room before I could watch TV the other night. I wanted to wait until the next day to clean my room, but I did it when he said to so I could watch my favourite show.

How did that work out for you, Warimu?

Well, because I did what he said, he let me watch the show. Even more surprising, my dad watched it with me and was pretty cool about it.

So, how did you do that? I mean, what were you thinking that helped you to do what you didn't want to do?

I wanted to watch TV. Cleaning my room was the only way that was going to make it happen.

So you reminded yourself of the outcomes. That helped you get past your own preference to clean your room when it was more convenient for you, and to clean it when your dad wanted it to be done?

Yeah, I guess so.

That sounds pretty wise to me, Warimu. You looked at the outcome you wanted to achieve and you made up your mind, even though you didn't feel like it, to do what your dad wanted.

I suppose that's what I did.

> You didn't have to clean your room at that time, did you? But you did it because you were aiming for a goal. Right?
>
> Yes. That's right.

I wonder what would happen if you thought that way about Mrs. Smith's maths class— if you reminded yourself of your goal. There's nothing spiritual about the way to solve a maths problem, right? But one way, the teacher's way, might be wisest and help you get you what you want in that class.

I hadn't thought of it like that.

Well, why not experiment with it and see what happens? Remind yourself of your goal in that class—to pass with a good grade—and what you can do to get to that goal. That's what you did with your dad, right?

I can do that.

Give it a whirl and see what happens. Talk to yourself about your goals when you sit down to do homework and see if that makes it easier to do things the way Mrs. Smith wants them done.

Warimu left upbeat, hopeful, and with a sense of control about her maths situation. She thanked me for taking the time and said she'd let me know what happened.

The next day I looked Warimu up and we talked about maths class. Warimu said she had reminded herself about her goal and had done the homework the way Mrs. Smith wanted it to be done. And she gained the full credit lost in earlier assignments.

The Heart of the Situation

The connection I had made with Warimu allowed me to move to the next level of her motivation—her heart. We continued our discussion.

Warimu, may I change the subject a little?

Sure.

This is a kind of personal question, and if you'd rather not answer it, just say so and I'll exit quickly. Do you think there's a deeper reason why you eventually cleaned your room for your dad and why you responded to Mrs Smith's directions about homework?

I don't know.

Warimu, a while back you told me that you know the Lord. Tell me about your relationship with Christ. How important is it to you?

From this point on in the conversation, I had the opportunity to explore the effect that Warimu's professed relationship with Christ had on her motives and actions. We talked about the sins of stubbornness and wilfulness, the reason for honouring those in authority, and how to disagree with authority figures respectfully. Warimu's "wise want" to succeed fuelled the initial interchange between Warimu and me, but it also led to her willingness to consider heart matters.

Youth workers can substitute any number of things they hear from teenagers for Mrs. Smith's "unreasonable" maths requirement: Mum and Dad's restriction of phone use, instant messaging, or computer time; Dad's refusal to let his son use the car when his homework is not done, being grounded if she doesn't come in when she's told to; getting detentions when he is late for school lots of mornings; being blamed by the teacher for disrupting class—even when he's not the one making noise. The list goes on.

No matter what the issue, after a counsellor connects with a teenager by talking about his or her goals, he can focus on solutions mind from the teenager's own past experiences, but then move counselling toward the heart needs that God says must be addressed.

This all may not happen in one meeting, but our Church and Christian school contexts allow counselling to be an ongoing informal relationship. Everything does not have to be said all at one time. Jesus modelled this pacing with His disciples. He said, "I have much more to say to you, more than you can now bear" (John 16:12). In short, this outside-to-the inside pattern, as people have ears to hear, seems to be God's pattern of working with spiritually indifferent or self-absorbed people—especially youth.

CHAPTER NINE

WHEN GOOD CHILDREN MAKE BAD CHOICES
WHY DO CHILDREN TURN OUT THE WAY THEY DO?

A. Does good parenting guarantee good children?

Proverbs 22:6 Train up a child in the way he should go and when he is old he will not depart from it.

1. Is Proverbs 22:6 an unconditional promise or a maxim?
2. There is no guarantee of success. We are dependent upon God's sovereign grace.
   a. None of us is a good enough parent to merit our child's salvation! Hebrews 12:10
   b. Our children are so sinful they would reject discipline; Genesis. 8:21

B. God blesses faithful parents.

1. Discipline may spare your children from death; Proverbs. 23:13-14
2. Your children will bring you joy; Proverbs. 29:17

C. If you neglect discipline you will contribute to your child's ruin and your own misery: a matter of life and death.

1. Learn from Eli and David; I Samuel. 2:12-17, 22-25 3:13 4:11 I Kings 1:5-6
2. Children die of parental neglect; Proverbs 20:20; 30:17 Exodus. 21:15, 17

3. Other parents try hard, but fail because they use the wrong method.
   4. Bad patterns established in childhood last a lifetime.
   5. Parents suffer grief and shame; Proverbs. 17:21, 25 29:15b 19:13. The father of a fool has no joy. A foolish son is a grief to his father and bitterness to her who bore him

D. Children are responsible for the choices they make; Proverbs 20:11 Ezekiel 18:5-13 It is by his deeds that a lad distinguishes himself.

   1. Not all rebellion is the fault of the parents.
   2. What was the difference between Cain and Abel? Genesis 4:1-9
      a. Both were born with the same fallen nature.
      b. Both grew up in the same environment.
      c. Neither had the wicked influences our kids face.
      d. Each was responsible for the choice he made.
   3. Israel, like Cain, rejected God's discipline; Jeremiah 2:30 5:3 7:28
   4. If you reject discipline, you will die young; Proverbs 20:20 30:11, 17
   5. Foolishness in childhood can last a lifetime.
   6. If you respect and obey your parents, you will live and prosper; Ephesians.6:2 Exodus 20:12

E. You can't save your children!

How can parents prevent their children from getting out of control?

A. Discipline them while there is hope; Ephesians 6:4

1. Why is discipline necessary? Genesis 8:21; Psalms. 51:5; Proverbs 22:15
2. How should discipline be carried out? The Process:
   a. You must be self-disciplined.
   b. Teach principles of behaviour from the Bible.
   c. Don't merely target behaviour. Deal with the heart of sin Proverbs 4:23; Mark. 7:20-23
   d. Demand immediate and respectful obedience.
   e. When the rules are broken take disciplinary action. Proverbs 22:15; 29:15; 13:24
   f. Lovingly forgive and restore the relationship; I John 1:9
   g. Point them to their need of redemption in Christ.
3. Questions about discipline.
   a. Why not use time outs and other methods favoured by modern psychologists? Proverbs 22:15; 19:18; Colossians 2:8-9
   b. But I love my child too much to spank him/her Proverbs 23:13-14; 13:24; 19:18

      c. Are there times when other forms of discipline should be used? Exodus 22:1

      d. Is there a legitimate place for rewards for obedience? Ephesians 6:2-3

      e. What about children diagnosed with ADD or ADHD?

      f. What about disciplining older children (teenagers)?

4. Discipline is hard work (love)! Don't lose heart; Hebrews 12:6-9 you are disciplining them on the Lord's behalf.

B. Train them in the Word. Deuteronomy 6:4-9; 20-25; Proverbs 6:20-23

  1. Parents are responsible for the education of their children. Proverbs 6:20-23

      a. The primary place of training is the home.

      b. Children need to understand all of reality from the perspective of Scripture.

      c. You are to prepare your children to live as God's people in the world.

      d. You cannot delegate the education of your children to anyone else.

      e. Make your family the primary influence in your child's life.

  2. You must instruct your children. Deuteronomy 6:4-9; 20-25

a. The Word must first be on your heart! Deuteronomy 6:4-6
   b. Train them through formal teaching: family worship Deuteronomy 6:7; II Titus 3:15
   c. Train your children through informal instruction.
   Deuteronomy 6:9; 20-25
   d. Prepare them for adult life.
   e. Strive to build an intimate relationship with your children. Proverbs 20:5
3. Evangelize your children. Deuteronomy 6:20-25

Incorporate the gospel into the way you train your children.

C. Don't provoke them to anger (or drive them to rebellion). Colossians 3:21

   1. Over discipline I John 5:3
      a. Unrealistic demands and expectations. I Thessalonians 2:11 I Colossians 13:11
      b. Overprotection: Not letting children grow up. Luke 12:48 I Colossians 13:11
      c. Anger/harshness: verbal or physical abuse. Js. 1:19-20 Matthew 5:21-23
      d. Humiliation and ridicule. Matthew 18:15a Ephesians 4:29

- **e.** Refusal to listen. Proverbs 18:3, 17; Ephesians 4:25 Joshua 1:19; Proverbs 20:5; Deuteronomy 6:20
- **f.** False accusations, fault finding and negativity; Proverbs 19:11
- **g.** Failure to encourage and reward good behaviour; Colossians. 3:21 Revelations; 2-3; I Colossians; 1:1f
- **h.** Failure to express unconditional and deep love. Psalms 103:13-14

2. Under discipline. Proverbs 19:18; I Samuel. 3:13

- **a.** Lack of boundaries and failure to enforce standards; Proverbs 29:15
- **b.** Threats not carried out.
- **c.** Overindulgence and enabling sinful behaviour.
- **d.** A child centred home.

3. Using worldly methodologies instead of the Bible!

- **a.** Behaviourism: Seeking to control behaviour without addressing the heart.
- **b.** Pharisaical works based discipline. – having the appearance of doing good, without engaging the heart.
- **c.** Stressing self-esteem; II Titus 3:1-2.
- **d.** Misplaced parental values and priorities

4. Other ways to frustrate and embitter your children include inconsistency, favouritism, comparison, hypocrisy, broken promises, lack of marital harmony, neglect, selfishness. Genesis 25:28 Matthew 5:23-24, 37 Psalms 15:4 Colossians 3:9 Ephesians. 5:22-33 II Samuel 14:28

What should parents do when their children rebel?

A. First deal with yourself.

1. Confess your own sinful failures; Proverbs 13:24 23:13-14 Colossians 3:21 Matthew 7: 1f 5:23-24
2. Recognize the sin of your child for what it is; Proverbs 22:15a
3. Seek godly counsel; Proverbs 11:14 15:22 20:18
4. Be prepared to face the reality that your child may not be a believer.
5. Pray and fast. Only God can change a rebellious heart of a child (or a parent) Matthew 17:21; Mark 9:29

B. Take care of the rest of your family.

1. Ensure you and your spouse are in agreement.
2. Watch out for your other children.

C. Mount a discipline offensive.

1. Be prepared to do some investigation.
2. Remove bad influences from his life. Proverbs 1:10f 13:20; Matthew 5:29-30; I Colossians 15:33
3. Establish clear and reasonable expectations.

- **a.** Curfew; Proverbs 2:13 7:9; I Thessalonians 5:7
- **b.** Entertainment standards: TV, movies, music, computer (internet/games). Proverbs 5:8; Romans 13:14; Ephesians 5:3
- **c.** Manner of listening and speaking to parents. Proverbs 19:26 20:20 30:17 Exodus 20:12
- **d.** Church involvement; Proverbs 8:1f; Hebrews 10:24-25
- **e.** Treatment of siblings Proverbs 18:6 12:16; Philippians 2:3-4
- **f.** Substance abuse; Proverbs 23:29-35 20:1; Ephesians 5:18
- **g.** Work/school performance (Not to remain idle); Proverbs 6:6-11
- **h.** Contribution to family: chores, finances, etc. Proverbs 10:5; Ephesians 4:28
- **i.** Participation in family activities (including family worship). Proverbs 1:8; Deuteronomy 6:7
- **j.** Companions/use of phone; Proverbs 13:20, 14:7 22:24; I Colossians 15:33
- **k.** Dress code Deuteronomy 22:5

4. Define and enforce consequences. Proverbs 23:13-14, 19:18

5. Appeal to your child on a heart level. Proverbs 22:15 2:2, 10 3:1, 3 4:23 6:21 11:20 14:14, 19:3 28:26 1:7; Mark 7:21f

6. It may be wise to have your child examined by a physician to see if there are physiological elements complicating the situation.
7. Don't undermine your own efforts.
   a. Both parents must be of one mind.
   b. Don't make empty threats and don't allow yourself to be manipulated!

D. Mount a love offensive.

1. Make it clear that your love is unconditional Matthew. 5:44-45; I John 4:19
2. Find ways to demonstrate your affection to your children without compromising your standards.
3. Be ready to forgive.
4. Never give up!

How you can handle difficult children?

In handling difficult children, the following points as well as scriptural references should be considered; Proverbs 19:18 29:1 Deuteronomy. 21:18f Exodus 21:15 Leviticus. 20:9

A. Beware of two extremes.

1. Giving up too soon because of personal hurt feelings, anger and bitterness.
2. Tolerating and enabling sin.

B. Under the Old Covenant, out of control (incorrigible) children were put to death; Proverbs 19:18; Deuteronomy 21:18-21

1. Drastic measures were required to ensure the purity of the covenant community.
2. These are principles that are still current.
   a. It is possible for a child to be incorrigible (out of control).
   b. Children (minors) are held responsible for their sinful choices.
   c. We are to be concerned about the corrupting influence of an incorrigible child upon the church (and the home).
   d. We must be prepared to take drastic measures.
3. God finally reaches a point at which He deals with Israel this way; Jeremiah. 3:8 7:28

C. Applications Uunder the New Covenant.

1. Apostates and rebels are no longer executed by the covenant community.
2. Bring them before the church leaders: excommunication; I Corinthians 5:1f; Matthew18:15f
3. Bring them before the civil leaders: criminal penalties; Matthew 18:17
   i. The magistrate doesn't always do his job.
   ii. Parents sometimes wrongfully circumvent the criminal consequences of their children's behaviour.
4. Put them out of the house.
   i. After they are legal adults you can ask them to leave the family home.

- **ii.** If they are still minors, you are legally required to provide food, shelter, housing and education.
- **iii.** You may, however, send them to a disciplined and controlled environment where they will receive food and shelter.
- **iv.** Do this in love, not anger; Romans 12:18f

D. The goals of drastic measures.

1. Protection for those who remain: Proverbs 1:10f I Colossians 5:6
2. The Lord may even use this hardship, like church discipline, to drive your child to his senses. Proverbs 3:11-12; I Colossians 5:5

E. When they come home

1. Beware of being manipulated and becoming enablers of their sinful lifestyle.
2. The child must be repentant, Luke 15:18, 21; II Colossians 7:10-11; having learned the difference between worldly sorrow and Godly sorrow over sin.
3. He/she must be willing to follow the house rules (use of written contracts).

Concluding Applications

A. Both parents and children are responsible; Proverbs 23:13-16

B. There is hope for failed parents and rebellious children; Luke 15:17-20

Helping Families with (Grown children who don't leave home)

I. INTRODUCTION.

Sometimes referred to as "Twixters" – these are adult children who don't leave home; some are grown-ups who refuse to take on adult responsibilities even though they want to be treated as adults.

II. WHY ARE THERE SO MANY TWIXTERS?

A. There are legitimate reasons for grown children to remain with their parents.

   i. A son may stay at home while he is completing his education, establishing his business, or saving for marriage.
   ii. A daughter may choose to stay under the protection of her parents prior to marriage; Genesis 2:24
   iii. Some young adults are not able to take care of themselves: i.e. disabilities.
   iv. Children may stay at home in order to take care of aged or disabled parents or other family members; Exodus 20:12
   v. Sometimes children move home because of other extraordinary circumstances.

B. Some young people are sinfully postponing the responsibilities of adulthood.

   i. They fail to establish a career by which they can provide for themselves; Proverbs 6:5-11; 12:11; 28:19; 16:26

- ii. They expect others to take care of their financial needs. II Thessalonians 3:10-13; I Timothy 5:8
- iii. They are financially irresponsible; Proverbs 22:7
- iv. They place a high value on social relationships and entertainment. Proverbs 14:23
- v. Instead of marrying and having a family, they indulge in uncommitted relationships and fornication; I Corinthians 6:9-10; 7:9; II Titus. 2:22

C. Parents contribute to this problem.

- i. They fail to prepare their children for adult life; Proverbs 1:8
- ii. Some refuse to let go of their children; Genesis 2:24
- iii. They inadvertently finance and enable sinful behaviour.
- iv. They are afraid to take strong steps to deal with their children; I Samuel 2:12f

III. STEPS PARENTS CAN TAKE TO PREPARE THEIR CHILDREN TO LIVE AS RESPONSIBLE ADULTS

A. It is the job of parents, not schools or churches to train children; Proverbs 1:8-9

B. The goal of parenting is to make your children ready to live wisely; Genesis 2: 2 4; Proverbs 4:3-4; I Corinthians 13:11. The whole book of Proverbs is written to this end.

1. Teach them to fear God and to live for his glory; Proverbs 1:7; 3:7-8 Deuteronomy 6:5; Matthew 22:37

2. Teach them to put others ahead of themselves; Matthew 22:39; Philippians. 2:3-4
3. Prepare them to pursue a vocation so they can work hard to care for a family; Proverbs 6:5-11; 24:30-34; 26:12-16; 12:11; 13:11; 22:29; 10:4-5; 28:19 14:23
4. Teach them financial wisdom.
    i. The value of saving (postponed gratification); Proverbs 6:8; 13:11
    ii. The importance of budgeting (planning); Proverbs 21:5
    iii. Avoiding debt; Proverbs 22:7; 6:1-5; Deuteronomy 28:44
    iv. The prompt payment of financial obligations. Proverbs 3:27-28; Deuteronomy 24:14f; Psalms 37:21
    v. The blessedness of being generous; Proverbs 3:9-10; 11:25; 19:17; 22:9
5. Teach them God's design for marriage (and sex); Proverbs 5:1-23; 6:20-35 7:1-27
    i. Teach them biblical perspectives on manhood and womanhood; Proverbs 31:10f
    ii. Warn them against immorality; Proverbs 2:16-19
    iii. Encourage them to get ready for marriage; I Corinthians 7:9

6. Teach them to choose their companions carefully; Proverbs 1:10-19; 13:20; 22:24-25; 23:20; I Corinthians 15:33; Psalms 1:1

7. Teach them to resist temptation. Proverbs 29:25 2:12-15 20:1 31:4-5

C. When is a child ready to leave home? I Corinthians 13:11.

1. Spiritual maturity necessary to lead a wife and children.

2. Personal maturity is necessary to be a responsible husband and father; Ephesians 5:22f

3. Economic maturity is necessary to keep a job and handle money.

4. Physical maturity is necessary to work and protect a family; Proverbs 6:6f

5. Sexual maturity is important for marriage and to fulfil God's purposes; II Titus 2:22

6. Moral maturity is necessary to lead as an example of righteousness.

7. Ethical maturity is necessary to make responsible decisions.

8. Worldview maturity is necessary to understand what is really important.

9. Relational maturity is necessary to understand and respect others; Philippians 2:3-4

10. Social maturity is necessary to make a contribution to society; Matthew 5:13; Romans 13:1f

11. Verbal maturity is necessary to communicate and articulate as a man; Proverbs 15:28; 10:20-21; 16:24; 12:18

12. Character maturity is necessary to demonstrate courage under fire; Proverbs 29:25

13. Biblical maturity is necessary to lead at some level in the church; I Peter 4:10-11

IV. WHAT CAN PARENTS DO TO HELP THEIR TWIXTERS GROW UP?

A. Be willing to make tough choices for the good of your children.

1. If they continue to act like children, they must be treated like children.

2. Make your expectations clear, along with the consequences; possibly by introducing a written contract taking into account the desired outcomes of the parties concerned.

3. You may need to seek their forgiveness for spoiling them.

4. Their return to your home may be one last hope for you to train them; Proverbs 19:18

B. Combat sinful irresponsibility.

1. Force them to take financial responsibility.

2. Don't allow them to be lazy while living under your roof; Ephesians 4:28

3. Demand sexual purity.

4. Do not tolerate substance abuse.

5. Help them to learn from their mistakes.

C. What kind of help should you give your young adults?

   1. Just because you can afford to "help" them doesn't mean you will be doing them any good.
   2. Do not enable a lifestyle of laziness and sin.
   3. When you do offer help (i.e. educational expenses) demand a clear standard of responsibility and performance.

D. Do what you can to show you love them without compromising your standards.

V. WHAT CAN YOUNG PEOPLE DO TO PREPARE THEMSELVES FOR ADULT LIFE?

A. Seek wisdom from your parents; Proverbs 13:1; 6:20-23; 1:8, strive to bring them joy; Proverbs 23:24-25; 17:25

B. Find other Godly mentors who will help you to mature.

C. Learn to live for God and others, rather than being self-focused.

CHAPTER TEN

CLOSING REMARKS

As illustrated in this book, juvenile delinquency covers a multitude of violations of legal and social norms, ranging from minor offences to serious crimes committed by young people. Some types of juvenile delinquency constitute part of the process of maturation and growth and disappear spontaneously as young people make the transition to adulthood. Many socially responsible adults committed various types of petty offences during their adolescence.

Quite often, however, the situation is far more serious. Poverty, social exclusion and unemployment often cause marginalization, and young people who are marginalized are more susceptible to developing and maintaining delinquent behaviour. Furthermore, young people are more likely to become victims of crimes committed by juvenile delinquents. Delinquency is largely a group phenomenon; it is frequently engaged in by certain subcultures of young people who have jointly assumed a particular identity. It is also primarily a male phenomenon, with crime rates for male juvenile and young adult offenders more than double those for females. Some criminal activities are associated with intolerance of members of other cultures or religious, racial or ethnic groups. If delinquency policies are to be truly effective, higher priority must be given to marginalized, vulnerable and disadvantaged young people in society, and issues relating to youth in conflict with the law should be a central focus of national youth policies.

<u>When counselling **the adolescent, the counsellor must first get into the business of building rapport**</u>. Time must be spent to build rapport and a good relationship with the youth. The counsellor must create a receptive atmosphere so the adolescent knows you are willing to listen to him, that you are going to be sensitive and open to what he (she) has to say. Honesty and respect mixed with gentle firmness must be maintained. The counsellor must deal directly with resistance and confront the young person about it. Let him know when he is developing a resistant attitude and allow him to express himself but keep things progressing. You must keep things on a conversational level, focus on discussion and concrete issues. Periodically take the time to summarize or point out what is happening emotionally within the counselling session and always listen to the adolescent, giving him (or her) the right and the responsibility for giving feedback about what is going on.

Solomon, in his proverbial counsel, presumes that motives are a part of us, even though we may not be aware of them. "A man's ways seem right to him but motives are judged by the LORD" (Proverbs 18:3). We all act, we all have thoughts about our actions, and we all have motives for our actions and thoughts. This verse does not give carte blanche approval to all motives. In fact, all our motives are contaminated by sin. But at this deeper level, because of God's creation and common grace, other Biblical testimony assumes that some of our motives contain some measure of wisdom.

We can fruitfully counsel young people who are committed to their wants by detecting and affirming their underlying "wise wants." These are the desires, motives, longings and wants that God has created as part of our human nature. For sure, it is ultimately God's purposes that the teenager needs to pursue. It is God's truth that will set the teenager free. It is also the teenager's common self-centredness that distorts his perspective about his problems and the real solutions to them.

God's approach to young people, as pictured in the wisdom (bible) literature, shows that the young person's interests are wise starting places for the counsellor. In Proverbs, wise counsel to angry, foolish, or indifferent young people begins with apparent solutions to the desires and goals they already have. The vast majority of the proverbs make certain assumptions about the motivations of young adults. "Lazy hands make a man poor, but diligent hands bring wealth" (Proverbs 10:4), this assumes that teenagers want to avoid poverty and acquire wealth. "A man is praised according to his wisdom, but men with warped minds are despised" (Proverbs 12:8), this assumes that young people want praise, approval, and respect and do not want the opposite. These desires are "wise wants."

"Wise wants" inform the counsel in Proverbs. Presumably, youth desire to have a reputation for trustworthiness and honour, they desire to have parents who are proud and joyful because of them, healthy friendships, delightful romance, a sense of security and confidence, usefulness in the lives of others, and competence and success in work. Other proverbs assume that young people want to be discerning and thoughtful; to use good judgment to be able to respond effectively to the questions and demands of others, to combat laziness, selfishness, anger, lying, and lust, and to not be seduced, exploited, deceived or misled. God has programmed these desires, or "wise wants" into teenagers—into all of us. Counsel to young people can build upon these wants the same way Proverbs' crisp counsel does. But youth counsellors must first of all identify the teenager's "wise wants," then see how these wise wants have been distorted by the folly of youthfulness.

Parents and other authorities often react to the teenager's foolish choices and miss his "wise wants." This confusion is furthered by the faulty assumption that what the teenager wants—as reflected in his immediate choices, words, or patterns of behaviour—is what he really wants. But most teenagers do not see where their choices lead. They do not live with an "eschatological perspective"—the big picture of how their decisions impact their future and God's purposes for them. They are here-and-now people, just as Proverbs assumes them to be. The counsellor has to be geared to listen for the "wise want," now distorted into foolish desires that direct the young person's choices.

CHAPTER ELEVEN

UNITED NATIONS GUIDELINES FOR THE PREVENTION OF JUVENILE DELINQUENCY (THE RIYADH GUIDELINES)

Adopted and proclaimed by General Assembly resolution 45/112 of December 14, 1990

I. FUNDAMENTAL PRINCIPLES

- The prevention of juvenile delinquency is an essential part of crime prevention in society. By engaging in lawful, socially useful activities and adopting a humanistic orientation towards society and outlook on life, young persons can develop non-criminogenic attitudes.
- The successful prevention of juvenile delinquency requires efforts on the part of the entire society to ensure the harmonious development of adolescents, with respect for and promotion of their personality from early childhood.
- For the purposes of the interpretation of the present Guidelines, a child-centred orientation should be pursued. Young persons should have an active role and partnership within society and should not be considered as mere objects of socialization or control.
- In the implementation of the present Guidelines, in accordance with national legal systems, the well-being of young persons from their early childhood should be the focus of any preventive programme.

- The need for and importance of progressive delinquency prevention policies and the systematic study and the elaboration of measures should be recognized. These should avoid criminalizing and penalizing a child for behaviour that does not cause serious damage to the development of the child or harm to others. Such policies and measures should involve:

a. The provision of opportunities, in particular educational opportunities, to meet the varying needs of young persons and to serve as a supportive framework for safeguarding the personal development of all young persons, particularly those who are demonstrably endangered or at social risk and are in need of special care and protection

b. Specialized philosophies and approaches for delinquency prevention, on the basis of laws, processes, institutions, facilities and a service delivery network aimed at reducing the motivation, need and opportunity for, or conditions giving rise to, the commission of infractions

c. Official intervention to be pursued primarily in the overall interest of the young person and guided by fairness and equity

d. Safeguarding the well-being, development, rights and interests of all young persons

e. Consideration that youthful behaviour or conduct that does not conform to overall social norms and values is often part of the maturation and growth process, and tends to disappear spontaneously in most individuals with the transition into adulthood

f. Awareness that, in the predominant opinion of experts, labelling a young person as "deviant", "delinquent" or "pre-delinquent" often contributes to the development of a consistent pattern of undesirable behaviour.

- Community-based services and programmes should be developed for the prevention of juvenile delinquency, particularly where no agencies have yet been established. Formal agencies of social control should only be utilized as a means of last resort.

II. Scope of the Guidelines

- The present Guidelines should be interpreted and implemented within the broad framework of the Universal Declaration of Human Rights, the International Covenant on Economic, Social and Cultural Rights, the International Covenant on Civil and Political Rights, the Declaration of the Rights of the Child and the Convention on the Rights of the Child, and in the context of the United Nations Standard Minimum Rules for the Administration of Juvenile Justice (The Beijing Rules), as well as other instruments and norms relating to the rights, interests and well-being of all children and young persons.
- The present Guidelines should also be implemented in the context of the economic, social and cultural conditions prevailing in each Member State.

III. GENERAL PREVENTION
- Comprehensive prevention plans should be instituted at every level of Government and include the following:
  a. In-depth analyses of the problem and inventories of programmes, services, facilities and resources available
  b. Well-defined responsibilities for the qualified agencies, institutions and personnel involved in preventive efforts
  c. Mechanisms for the appropriate co-ordination of prevention efforts between governmental and non-governmental agencies
  d. Policies, programmes and strategies based on prognostic studies to be continuously monitored and carefully evaluated in the course of implementation
  e. Methods for effectively reducing the opportunity to commit delinquent acts
  f. Community involvement through a wide range of services and programmes
  g. Close interdisciplinary co-operation between national, State, provincial and local governments, with the involvement of the private sector, representative citizens of the community to be served, and labour, child-care, health education, social, law enforcement and judicial agencies in taking concerted action to prevent juvenile delinquency and youth crime

h. Youth participation in delinquency prevention policies and processes, including recourse to community resources, youth self-help, and victim compensation and assistance programmes

i. Specialized personnel at all levels

IV. SOCIALIZATION PROCESSES

- Emphasis should be placed on preventive policies facilitating the successful socialization and integration of all children and young persons, in particular through the family, the community, peer groups, schools, vocational training and the world of work, as well as through voluntary organizations. Due respect should be given to the proper personal development of children and young persons, and they should be accepted as full and equal partners in socialization and integration processes.

A. Family

1. Every society should place a high priority on the needs and well-being of the family and of all its members.

2. Since the family is the central unit responsible for the primary socialization of children, governmental and social efforts to preserve the integrity of the family, including the extended family, should be pursued. The society has a responsibility to assist the family in providing care and protection and in ensuring the physical and mental well-being of children. Adequate arrangements including day-care should be provided.

3. Governments should establish policies that are conducive to the bringing up of children in stable and settled family environments. Families in need of assistance in the resolution of conditions of instability or conflict should be provided with requisite services.

4. Where a stable and settled family environment is lacking and when community efforts to assist parents in this regard have failed, and the extended family cannot fulfil this role, alternative placements, including foster care and adoption, should be considered. Such placements should replicate, to the extent possible, a stable and settled family environment, while, at the same time, establishing a sense of permanence for children, thus avoiding problems associated with "foster drift".

5. Special attention should be given to children of families affected by problems brought about by rapid and uneven economic, social and cultural change, in particular the children of indigenous, migrant and refugee families. As such changes may disrupt the social capacity of the family to secure the traditional rearing and nurturing of children, often as a result of role and culture conflict, innovative and socially constructive modalities for the socialization of children have to be designed.

6. Measures should be taken and programmes developed to provide families with the

opportunity to learn about parental roles and obligations as regards child development and child care, promoting positive parent-child relationships, sensitizing parents to the problems of children and young persons and encouraging their involvement in family and community-based activities.

7. Governments should take measures to promote family cohesion and harmony and to discourage the separation of children from their parents, unless circumstances affecting the welfare and future of the child leave no viable alternative.

8. It is important to emphasize the socialization function of the family and extended family; it is also equally important to recognize the future role, responsibilities, participation and partnership of young persons in society.

9. In ensuring the right of the child to proper socialization, Governments and other agencies should rely on existing social and legal agencies, but, whenever traditional institutions and customs are no longer effective, they should also provide and allow for innovative measures.

B. Education

1. Governments are under an obligation to make public education accessible to all young persons.

2. Education systems should, in addition to their academic and vocational training activities, devote particular attention to the following:

a. Teaching of basic values and developing respect for the child's own cultural identity and patterns, for the social values of the country in which the child is living, for civilizations different from the child's own and for human rights and fundamental freedoms

b. Promotion and development of the personality, talents and mental and physical abilities of young people to their fullest potential

c. Involvement of young persons as active and effective participants in, rather than mere objects of, the educational process

d. Undertaking activities that foster a sense of identity with and of belonging to the school and the community

e. Encouragement of young persons to understand and respect diverse views and opinions, as well as cultural and other differences

f. Provision of information and guidance regarding vocational training, employment opportunities and career development

g. Provision of positive emotional support to young persons and the avoidance of psychological maltreatment

h. Avoidance of harsh disciplinary measures, particularly corporal punishment

3. Educational systems should seek to work together with parents, community organizations and agencies concerned with the activities of young persons.

4. Young persons and their families should be informed about the law and their rights and responsibilities under the law, as well as the universal value system, including United Nations instruments.

5. Educational systems should extend particular care and attention to young persons who are at social risk. Specialized prevention programmes and educational materials, curricula, approaches and tools should be developed and fully utilized.

6. Special attention should be given to comprehensive policies and strategies for the prevention of alcohol, drug and other substance abuse by young persons. Teachers and other professionals should be equipped and trained to prevent and deal with these problems. Information on the use and abuse of drugs, including alcohol, should be made available to the student body.

7. Schools should serve as resource and referral centres for the provision of medical, counselling, and other services to young persons, particularly those with special needs and suffering from abuse, neglect, victimization and exploitation.

8. Through a variety of educational programmes, teachers and other adults and the student body should be sensitized to the problems, needs and perceptions of young persons, particularly those belonging to underprivileged, disadvantaged, ethnic or other minority and low-income groups.

9. School systems should attempt to meet and promote the highest professional and educational standards with respect to curricula, teaching and learning methods and approaches, and the recruitment and training of qualified teachers. Regular monitoring and assessment of performance by the appropriate professional organizations and authorities should be ensured.

10. School systems should plan, develop and implement extracurricular activities of interest to young persons, in co-operation with community groups.

11. Special assistance should be given to children and young persons who find it difficult to comply with attendance codes, and to "drop-outs".

12. Schools should promote policies and rules that are fair and just; students should be represented in bodies formulating school policy, including policy on discipline, and decision-making.

C. Community

1. Community-based services and programmes which respond to the special needs, problems, interests and concerns of young persons and which offer appropriate counselling and guidance to young persons and their families should be developed, or strengthened where they exist.

2. Communities should provide, or strengthen where they exist, a wide range of community-based support measures for young persons, including community development centres, recreational facilities and services to respond to the special problems of children who are at social risk. In providing these helping measures, respect for individual rights should be ensured.

3. Special facilities should be set up to provide adequate shelter for young persons who are no longer able to live at home or who do not have houses to live in.

4. A range of services and helping measures should be provided to deal with the difficulties experienced by young persons in the transition to adulthood. Such services should include special programmes for young drug abusers which emphasize care, counselling, assistance and therapy-oriented interventions.

5. Voluntary organizations providing services for young persons should be given financial

and other support by Governments and other institutions.

6. Youth organizations should be created or strengthened at the local level and given full participatory status in the management of community affairs. These organizations should encourage youth to organize collective and voluntary projects, particularly projects aimed at helping young persons in need of assistance.

7. Government agencies should take special responsibility and provide necessary services for less disadvantaged or street children; information about local facilities, accommodation, employment and other forms and sources of help should be made readily available to young persons.

8. A wide range of recreational facilities and services of particular interest to young persons should be established and made easily accessible to them.

D. Mass media

1. The mass media should be encouraged to ensure that young persons have access to information and material from diverse national and international sources.

2. The mass media should be encouraged to portray the positive contribution of young persons to society.

3. The mass media should be encouraged to disseminate information on the existence of services, facilities and opportunities for young persons in society.

4. The mass media generally, and the television and film media in particular, should be encouraged to minimize the level of pornography, drugs and violence portrayed and to display violence and exploitation disfavourably, as well as encouraged to avoid demeaning and degrading presentations, especially of children, women and interpersonal relations, and to promote egalitarian principles and roles.

5. The mass media should be aware of its extensive social role and responsibility, as well as its influence, in communications related to youthful drug and alcohol abuse. It should use its power for drug abuse prevention by relaying consistent messages through a balanced approach. Effective drug awareness campaigns at all levels should be promoted.

E. Social Policy

1. Government agencies should give high priority to plans and programmes for young persons and should provide sufficient funds and other resources for the effective delivery of services, facilities and staff for adequate medical and mental health care, nutrition, housing and other relevant services, including drug and alcohol abuse prevention and treatment, ensuring that such resources reach and actually benefit young persons.

2. The institutionalization of young persons should be a measure of last resort and for the minimum necessary period, and the best interests of the young person should be of paramount importance. Criteria authorizing formal intervention of this type should be strictly defined and limited to the following situations: (a) where the child or young person has suffered harm that has been inflicted by the parents or guardians; (b) where the child or young person has been sexually, physically or emotionally abused by the parents or guardians; (c) where the child or young person has been neglected, abandoned or exploited by the parents or guardians; (d) where the child or young person is threatened by physical or moral danger due to the behaviour of the parents or guardians; and (e) where a serious physical or psychological danger to the child or young person has manifested itself in his or her own behaviour and neither the parents, the guardians, the juvenile himself or herself nor non-residential community services can meet the danger by any means other than institutionalization.

3. Government agencies should provide young persons with the opportunity of continuing in full-time education, funded by the State where parents or guardians are unable to support the young persons, and of receiving work experience.

4. Programmes to prevent delinquency should be planned and developed on the basis of reliable, scientific research findings, and periodically monitored, evaluated and adjusted accordingly.

5. Scientific information should be disseminated to the professional community and to the public at large about the sort of behaviour or situation

which indicates or may result in physical and psychological victimization, harm and abuse, as well as exploitation, of young persons.

6. Generally, participation in plans and programmes should be voluntary. Young persons themselves should be involved in their formulation, development and implementation.

7. Government should begin or continue to explore, develop and implement policies, measures and strategies within and outside the criminal justice system to prevent domestic violence against and affecting young persons and to ensure fair treatment to these victims of domestic violence.

F. Legislation and juvenile justice administration

1. Governments should enact and enforce specific laws and procedures to promote and protect the rights and well-being of all young persons.

2. Legislation preventing the victimization, abuse, exploitation and the use for criminal activities of children and young persons should be enacted and enforced.

3. No child or young person should be subjected to harsh or degrading correction or punishment measures at, in schools, or in any other institutions.

4. Legislation and enforcement aimed at restricting and controlling accessibility of weapons of any sort to children and young persons should be pursued.

5. In order to prevent further stigmatization, victimization and criminalization of young persons, legislation should be enacted to ensure that any conduct not considered an offence or not penalized if committed by an adult is not considered an offence and not penalized if committed by a young person.

6. Consideration should be given to the establishment of an office of ombudsman or similar independent organ, which would ensure that the status, rights and interests of young persons are upheld and that proper referral to available services is made. The ombudsman or other organization designated would also supervise the implementation of the Riyadh Guidelines, the Beijing Rules and the Rules for the Protection of Juveniles Deprived of their Liberty. The ombudsman or other organization would, at regular intervals, publish a report on the progress made and on the difficulties encountered in the implementation of the instrument. Child advocacy services should also be established.

7. Law enforcement and other relevant personnel, of both sexes, should be trained to respond to the special needs of young persons and should be familiar with and use, to the maximum extent possible, programmes and referral possibilities for the diversion of young persons from the justice system.

8. Legislation should be enacted and strictly enforced to protect children and young persons from drug abuse and drug traffickers.

G. Research, policy development and coordination

1. Efforts should be made and appropriate mechanisms established to promote, on multidisciplinary and an intradisciplinary basis, interaction and coordination between economic, social, education and health agencies and services, the justice system, youth, community and development agencies and other relevant institutions.
2. The exchange of information, experience and expertise gained through projects, programmes, practices and initiatives relating to youth crime, delinquency prevention and juvenile justice should be intensified at the national, regional and international levels.
3. Regional and international co-operation on matters of youth crime, delinquency prevention and juvenile justice involving practitioners, experts and decision makers should be further developed and strengthened.
4. Technical and scientific cooperation on practical and policy-related matters, particularly in training, pilot and demonstration projects, and on specific issues concerning the prevention of youth crime and juvenile delinquency should be strongly supported by all Governments, the United Nations system and other concerned organizations.
5. Collaboration should be encouraged in undertaking scientific research with respect to effective modalities for youth crime and juvenile delinquency prevention, and the findings of such

research should be widely disseminated and evaluated.

6. Appropriate United Nations bodies, institutions, agencies and offices should pursue close collaboration and coordination on various questions related to children juvenile justice and youth crime and juvenile delinquency prevention.

7. On the basis of the present Guidelines, the United Nations Secretariat, in cooperation with interested institutions, should play an active role in research, scientific collaboration, the formulation of policy options, and the review and monitoring of their implementation, and should serve as a source of reliable information on effective modalities for delinquency prevention.

REFERENCES

Adams, J. E. <u>Competent to Counsel</u>. Nutley NJ: Presbyterian and Reformed Publishing Co., 1977.

Adams, J. E. (1986). *How To Help People Change*. Grand Rapids: Zondervan.

Adams, K. (2003). The effectiveness of juvenile curfews at crime prevention. *Annals of the American Academy of Political and Social Science*, 587(136-159).

Airaksinen, T. (2004). Youth Rise. EUCPN Best practice award. Retrieved 03.11.2005, from **http://www.rikoksentorjunta.fi/uploads/ yyx1pjpihux0t.doc**

Alberola, C., & Molina, E. (2004). *Report of the Spanish Juvenile Justice System*. Albacete: University of Castilla La Mancha.

Anker, F. (2005). Starting Together: Early Childhood Intervention to support families and to prevent psycho-social problems in children 0—2 years (Sluitende aanpak voor 0—2 jarigen in Arnhem, Breda, Maastricht en Rheden). Unpublished report Netherlands Ministry of Justice: The Hague.

Aos, S. (2003). Costs and benefits of criminal justice and prevention programs. In H. Kury & J. Obergfell-Fuchs (Eds.), *Crime Prevention: New Approaches* (pp. 413-442). Mainz: Weisser Ring.

Arthur, R. (2005). Punishing Parents for the Crimes of their Children. *The Howard Journal of Criminal Justice, 44*(3), 233-253.

Avi Astor, R., H.A., M., Benbenishty, R., Marachi, R., & Rosemond, M. (2005). School Safety Interventions: Best Practices and Programs. *Children and Schools, 27*(1), 17-32.

B&A. (2000). *The Moroccan community fathers. Examples of a citizen's initiative.* Amsterdam: DWA.

Baas, N. J. (2005). *The effectiveness of young offender intervention programmes and intervention conditions that influence their effectiveness.* The Hague: WODC, Ministry of Justice.

Baginsky, W. (2004). Peer-mentoring in the UK. A guide for schools Retrieved 13.02.2006, from http://www.betterbehaviourscotland.gov.uk/uploads/UK%20PeerMediation.pdf

Balvig, F. (1999). *RisikoUngdom-Ungdomsundersøgelse 1999 [Youth at Risk-Youth Study]* København: Det Kriminalpræventive Balvig, F. (2001). *RisikoUngdom – Youth*

Backus, W., & Chapian, M. (2000). *Telling Yourself the Truth.* Bloomington: Bethany House.

Bibb, M. (1967). "Gang-Related Services of Mobilization for Youth." In M. W. Klein (ed.), Juvenile Gangs in Context: Theory,

Research, and Action (pp. 175–182). Englewood Cliffs, NJ: Prentice-Hall.

Braga. A. A. (2004). Gun Violence Among Serious Young Offenders. Problem-Oriented Guides for Police. Problem-Specific Guides Series. No. 23. Washington, DC: Office of Community Oriented Policing Services.

Burch, J., and Kane, C. (1999). Implementing the OJJDP Comprehensive Gang Model. Fact Sheet #122. Washington, DC: U.S. Department of Justice, Office of Justice Programs, Office of Juvenile Justice and Delinquency Prevention.

Bursik, R. J., Jr., and Grasmick, H. G. (1993). Neighborhoods and Crime: The Dimensions of Effective Community Control. New York, NY: Lexington.

Cloward, R. A., and Ohlin, L. E. (1960). Delinquency and Opportunity: A Theory of Delinquent Gangs. New York, NY: The Free Press.

Cohen, M. I., Williams, K., Bekelman, A. M., and Crosse, S. (1995). "Evaluation of the National Youth Gang Drug Prevention Program." In M. W. Klein, C. L. Maxson, and J. Miller (eds.), The Modern Gang Reader (pp. 266–275). Los Angeles, CA: Roxbury.

Coolbaugh, K., and Hansel, C. J. (2000). "The Comprehensive Strategy: Lessons Learned From the Pilot Sites." Juvenile Justice Bulletin. Washington, DC:

U.S. Department of Justice, Office of Juvenile Justice and Delinquency Prevention.

Crabb, Larry; *Effective Biblical Counselling* (Grand Rapids, Michigan: Zondervan, 1977)

David Benner *Strategic Pastoral Counselling* (Grand Rapids, Michigan: Baker Books, 1992)

Crabb, L. (1977). *Effective Biblical Counseling: A Model for Helping Caring Christians Become Capable Counsellors.* Grand Rapids: Zondervan.

Dzikus, A. and L. Ochola, "Street children in sub-Saharan Africa: Kenya's experience", Habitat Debate, vol. 2, No. 2 (1996).

Hawkins, J. D. (1999). "Preventing Crime and Violence Through Communities That Care." European Journal on Crime Policy and Research, 7, 443–458.

Hawkins, J. D., Catalano, R. F., and Arthur, M. W. (2002). "Promoting Science-Based Prevention in Communities." Addictive Behaviors, 27, 951–976.

Hunter, A. J. (1985). "Private, Parochial, and Public School Orders: The Problem of Crime and Incivility in Urban Communities." In G. Suttles and M. N. Zald, The Challenge of Control: Citizenship and Institution Building in Modern Society. Norwood, NJ: Ablex Publishing.

Hill, R. B. (1997). The Strengths of African American Families: Twenty-Five Years Later. Washington, DC: R & B Publishers.

Howell, J. C. (2003a). Preventing and Reducing Juvenile Delinquency: A Comprehensive Framework. Thousand Oaks, CA: Sage Publications.

——— (2003b). "Diffusing Research Into Practice Using the Comprehensive Strategy for Serious, Violent, and Chronic Juvenile Offenders." Youth Violence and Juvenile Justice: An Interdisciplinary Journal, 1(3), 219–245.

Hunter, A. J. (1985). "Private, Parochial, and Public School Orders: The Problem of Crime and Incivility in Urban Communities." In G. D. Suttles and M. N. Zald (eds.) The Challenge of Social Control: Citizenship and Institution Building in Modern Society (pp. 230–242). Norwood, NJ: Ablex Publishing.

Hearn, J. The Violences of Men: How Men Talk about and How Agencies Respond to Men's Violence to Women (London, Sage, 1998); L.A. Goodman and others, "Male violence against women", American Psychologist, vol. 48, No. 10 (1993), pp. 1,054-1,058; and M.P. Koss and others, No Safe Haven: Male Violence Against Women at Home, at Work and in the Community (Washington, American Psychological Association, 1994).

Kahn, A. J. (1967). "From Delinquency Treatment to Community Development." In P. F. Lazarsfeld, W. H. Sewell, and H. L. Wilensky (eds.), The Uses of Sociology (pp. 477–505). New York, NY: Basic Books.

Klein, M. W. (1971). Street Gangs and Street Workers. Englewood Cliffs, NJ: Prentice-Hall. Kornhauser, R. (1978). Social Sources of Delinquency. Chicago, IL: University of Chicago Press.

Klein, M. The American Street Gang: Its Nature, Prevalence, and Control (New York, Oxford University Press, 1995), pp. 138-139.

Lane, J., and Meeker, J. W. (2003). "Women's and Men's Fear of Gang Crimes: Sexual and Nonsexual Assault as Perceptually Contemporaneous Offenses."

Johnson, U.; Gang Violence Prevention: A Curriculum and Discussion Guide (Pleasantville, New York, Sunburst Communications, 1995).

MacArthur, J., F., Jr, Mack, W. A., Introduction to biblical counselling : Basic guide to the principles and practice of counselling (Electronic ed.) (55). Dallas, TX: Word Pub.

MacArthur, J., F., Jr, **Counselling: How to Counsel Biblically** 2005 Updated page 244ff 2005

McMinn, M. R. (1996). *Psychology, Theology, and Spirituality in Christian Counseling.* Forest: Tyndale House Publishers.

Ogefere, Tony, 1998-2011, Counselling Diary; unpublished

Roberts, A. R. (1989). <u>Juvenile Justice: Policies, Programs, and Services</u>. Chicago, IL: Dorsey Press.

Salazar, N. D., and Hatchell, B. S. (1990). <u>Rising Above Gangs and Drugs: How to Start a Community Reclamation Project</u>. Lomita, CA: Community Reclamation Project.

Sampson, R. J. (2002). "The Community." In J. Petersilia and J. Q. Wilson (eds.), <u>Crime: Public Policies for Crime Control</u> (pp. 225–252). Oakland, CA: Institute for Contemporary Studies Press.

Sampson, R. J., Raudenbush, S. W., and Earls, F. (1997). "Neighborhoods and Violent Crime: A Multilevel Study of Collective Efficacy." <u>Science</u>, 277, 918–924.

Schimke, D. (1999). "Where Others Fear to Tread." <u>Minneapolis/St. Paul City Pages</u>, 20(988). URL: **www.citypages.com/databank/20/988/article8167.asp**.

Schlossman, S., and Sedlak, M. (1983). <u>The Chicago Area Project Revisited</u>. Santa Monica, CA: Rand.

Shaw, C. R., and McKay, H. D. (1942/1972). <u>Juvenile Delinquency and Urban Areas</u>. Chicago, IL: University of Chicago Press.

Spergel, I. A. (1964). Racketville, Slumtown, Haulburg. Chicago: University of Chicago Press.

Spergel, I. The Youth Gang Problem (New York, Oxford University Press, 1995).

Tolman, J. and K. Pittman, with B. Cervone and others, Youth Acts, Community Impacts: Stories of Youth Engagement with Real Impacts, Community and Youth Development Series, vol. 7 (Takoma Park, Maryland, Forum for Youth Investment, 2001).

Venkatesh, S. "The social organization of street gang activity in an urban ghetto", American Journal of Sociology, vol. 103, No. 1 (July 1997), pp. 82-111.

Wolfgang, M.E.; T.P. Thornberry and R.M. Figlio, From Boy to Man, from Delinquency to Crime (Chicago, University of Chicago Press, 1987).

Germany, Federal Ministry of the Interior and Federal Ministry of Justice, "First periodical report on crime and crime control in Germany" (Berlin, July 2001).

Gilmore, D. Manhood in the Making: Cultural Concepts of Masculinity (London, Yale University Press, 1990).United Nations, "Report of the Tenth United Nations Congress on the Prevention of Crime and the Treatment of Offenders, Vienna, 10-17 April 2000" (A/CONF.187.15).

Organization of African Unity and UNICEF, "Africa's children, Africa's future", a background sectoral paper prepared for the OAU International Conference on Assistance to African Children, Dakar, 25-27 November 1992.

United Nations Guidelines for the Prevention of Juvenile Delinquency (The Riyadh Guidelines), adopted and proclaimed by General Assembly resolution 45/112 of 14 December 1990, available at **http://www.unhchr.ch/html/menu3/b/h_comp47.htm**.

United Nations, World Programme of Action for Youth to the Year 2000 and Beyond, adopted by General Assembly resolution 50/81 of 14 December 1995.

American Psychological Association, "Violence and youth: psychology's response", summary report of the APA Commission on Violence and Youth (Washington, D.C., 1993).

Urban Management Programme, "Streetchildren and gangs in African cities: guidelines for local authorities", Working Paper Series, No. 18 (May 2000), p. iii.

United Nations, Centre for Social Development and Humanitarian Affairs, "The global situation of youth in the 1990s: trends and prospects" (ST/CSDHA/21) (1993).

United Nations, Department of Public Information, News Coverage Service, "Effects of armed conflict, youth participation in economic development, media influence discussed at Lisbon Conference", press release: statement by Agung Laksono, Minister for Youth and Sport Affairs of Indonesia (Lisbon, 10 August 1998) (SOC/4468).

United Nations, Department of Public Information, News Coverage Service, "Need for inter-sectoral approach to fighting crime and illegal drugs stressed in Third Committee debate", press release: statement of Dulul Biswas, representative of Bangladesh (4 October 2000) (UNIS/GA/SHC/301).

United Nations, Centre for Social Development and Humanitarian Affairs, "The global situation of youth in the 1990s: trends and prospects"...

"Trends in juvenile violence in European countries", based on a presentation by Christian Pfeiffer, National Institute of Justice Research Preview Series (May 1998).

United Nations, Centre for Social Development and Humanitarian Affairs, "The global situation of youth in the 1990s: trends and prospects"...

United Nations, Department of Public Information, News Coverage Service, "Youth policies, empowerment, employment discussed at Lisbon World Conference", press release (12 August 1998) (SOC/4470).

Centre for the Protection of Women and Children, "Violence against women and children in Kosova", Regional Conference on Violence against Women and Children in Kosova, Pristina, 30 June to 2 July 2002.

United Nations Guidelines for the Prevention of Juvenile Delinquency (The Riyadh Guidelines)...

United Nations Guidelines for the Prevention of Juvenile Delinquency (The Riyadh Guidelines)...

State of Florida, "Key juvenile crime trends and conditions", available at myflorida.com, the official portal of the State of Florida (see http://www.djj.state. fl.us/ publicsafety/ learn /jjcrimetrends.html). 208

State of California, Department of Justice, Division of Law Enforcement, "Gang 2000: a call to action; the Attorney General's report on the impact of criminal street gangs on crime and prevention by the Year 2000" (Sacramento, 1993).

Urban Management Programme, "Streetchildren and gangs in African cities: guidelines for local authorities"..., pp. 26-37.

United Nations, "Draft plans of action for the implementation during the period 2001-2005 of the Vienna Declaration on Crime and Justice: meeting the challenges of the twenty-first century: report of the Secretary-General", tenth session of the Commission on Crime Prevention and Criminal Justice, Vienna, 8- 17 May 2001 (E/CN.15/2001/5).

United Nations, Department of Public Information, News Coverage Service, "New way needed to assist crime victims with compensation, rehabilitation, Third Committee told in third day of crime debate", press release: statement by Ruth Limjuco, representative of the Philippines (22 October 1996) (GA/SHC/3362).

United Nations, "Draft plans of action for the implementation during the period 2001-2005 of the Vienna Declaration on Crime and Justice: meeting the challenges of the twenty-first century: report of the Secretary-General"...

Introduction to Biblical Counselling

A Seminar to Equip Christian Leaders to Help People Using the All-Sufficient Scriptures 2006: Newheiser, Jim

The Billy Graham Christian Worker's Handbook; Edited by Charles G. Ward

1996 Worldwide Publications Minneapolis, Minnesota 55403

A Review of Good Practices in Preventing Juvenile Crime in the European Union

Prepared by Alex Stevens, Isabel Kessler and Ben Gladstone; February 2006

National Center for Neighborhood Enterprise (1999). Violence-Free Zone Initiatives. Washington, DC: National Center for Neighborhood Enterprise.

National Youth Gang Center (2002a). Assessing Your Community's Youth Gang Problem. Washington, DC: U.S. Department of Justice, Office of Juvenile Justice and Delinquency Prevention.

——— (2002b). Planning for Implementation of the OJJDP Comprehensive Gang Model. Washington, DC: U.S. Department of Justice, Office of Juvenile Justice and Delinquency Prevention.

Needle, J., and Stapleton, W. V. (1983). <u>Police Handling of Youth Gangs</u>. Washington, DC: U.S. Department of Justice, Office of Juvenile Justice and Delinquency Prevention.

Office of Juvenile Justice and Delinquency Prevention (2008). <u>Best Practices to Address Community Gang Problems: OJJDP's Comprehensive Gang Model</u>. Washington, DC: U.S. Department of Justice, Office of Justice Programs, Office of Juvenile Justice and Delinquency Prevention.

——— (1999). <u>Promising Strategies to Reduce Gun Violence</u>. Washington, DC: U.S. Department of Justice, Office of Justice Programs, Office of Juvenile Justice and Delinquency Prevention.